Waiting

Other Works By Elizabeth Swados

Literature

Nonfiction
At Play–2006
My Depression: A Picture Book–2005
The Four of Us–1991
Listening Out Loud–1988

Fiction
The Myth Man–1994
Flamboyant–1988
Leah and Lazar–1982

Poetry
The One and Only Human
Galaxy–2009

Children's Books
The Animal Rescue Store–2005
Hey You! C'mere!–2002
Dreamtective–1999
Inside Out–1990
Skydance–1981
Lullaby–1980
Girl with the Incredible Feeling–1976

Theater/Music

Broadway/Off-Broadway
Narcissus–2010
Kaspar Hauser–2009
Jabu–2005
Caucasian Chalk Circle–1998
The 49 Years–1997
Missionaries–1996
Prince and the Pauper–1994
Groundhog–1992
Jerusalem–1992

The Beautiful Lady–1985
Rap Master Ronnie–1984
Doonesbury–1982
The Haggadah–1980
Alice in Concert–1979
Dispatches–1979
Runaways–1978
The Good Woman of Setzuan–1976
The Greek Trilogy–1974
Nightclub Cantata–1973

Jewish Works
Atonement–2008
Jewish Girlz–2003
Judith–2001
Women of Valor–2001
Bible Women–1995
The Story of Job–1991
Jonah–1990
Song of Songs–1989
Esther, A Vaudeville Megillah–1988

Adolescent Theater and Education
Sosua–2010
Books Cook!–2010
Everyone Is Different–2007
Mental Missiles–2006
The Reality Show: NYU–2005 to 2011
Loss and Gain–2003
The Violence Project–2002
The Hating Pot–1997
The Red Sneaks–1989
Swing–1985

Waiting

Selected Nonfiction

Elizabeth Swados

Hanging Loose Press
Brooklyn, New York

Published by Hanging Loose Press, 231 Wyckoff Street, Brooklyn, New York 11217. All Rights Reserved. No part of this book may be reproduced without the publisher's written permission, except for brief quotations in reviews.

www.hangingloosepress.com

Printed in the United States of America
10 9 8 7 6 5 4 3 2 1

Hanging Loose thanks the Literature Program of the New York State Council on the Arts for a grant in support of the publication of this book.

Cover photograph by Carl Berg: The musée du quai Branly, Paris, reflection.

Drawings by Elizabeth Swados

Cover design by Marie Carter

Library of Congress Cataloging-in-Publication Data available on request.

ISBN: 978-1-934909-21-8

Table of Contents

for Ellen Stewart {1919-2011}

Introduction to *Waiting*

When selecting work for this collection, we have drawn on previously published magazine pieces and book chapters as well as much written especially for this book. Some of this was completed as 2011 opened and some decades before. Within these pages, Elizabeth Swados instructs those who would direct the young in plays, discusses musical composition, remembers those who have shaped her career and those who have passed through her life with far less impact. She shares painful experience and amusing incident. A woman who has done so much, traveled so widely, and felt so deeply does not make for easy encapsulation, but an attempt has been made here to capture both her intelligence and her compassion, her darkest moments and her wild sense of fun.

The reader may, of course, read this book from beginning to end or dip in and out as with any "selection." Our hope is that, however it is approached, *Waiting* will give not only pleasure and information but amazement that one woman could accomplish so much. Yes, she is known as a composer, director, teacher, children's book author, novelist, and poet, but Elizabeth Swados can also imitate singing styles from all over the world, set your poems to music, and advise you on dog care. She's got your back.

The Editors

I. Ellen

Why This Book Is for Ellen Stewart (2011)

Ellen Stewart was my mama for over thirty years and there is too much to say about her—for I've said it all. But I'd like to add here that in her eighties she began to direct and write her own pieces with the Great Jones Repertory Company. And she did them very well, received favorable reviews and toured them all over the world. I don't want to name them all but I know that she did *Oedipus*, *Dionysus*, and *Seven against Thebes* because I did the music for her. Also she did many, many other productions for which she was the composer as she discovered, again in her eighties, that she could write music. And she poured out songs to her dear musical director, Michael Sirotta, and he wrote them down. So, after giving space, productions, and nurturing to hundreds and hundreds of artists, Ellen now, herself, was an artist. She traveled everywhere from China to Japan to Albany to Croatia to Vienna and gave workshops as well as developed productions with the students with whom she worked. She loved her Great Jones Repertory Company in New York and used us all for her creations. Her works were visually stunning, with ten-foot-long puppets and horses that crossed the whole theater on wires, as well as shimmering hangings on all the walls, brilliant costumes, and dances inspired by the Japanese, Indonesian, Israeli, Arabic, Korean, Filipino, Italian, French, and other nationalities who make up our permanent company, which has grown over the years.

About 2006, her health began to fail, and after becoming very ill last year, she died on January 13, 2011. In her last years, several of her "babies" created a loft for her in the rehearsal space on Great Jones Street and set up a hospital bed and hired full-time rotating nurses to make sure she was safe. Now, right after her funeral mass at Saint Patrick's Cathedral, it seems a good time to reaffirm that Ellen was responsible for more than my career. She inspired me to work with young people and to give them a chance in the world. Not just on the stage. She encouraged me to travel and to understand that there is so much more than the New York artistic scene and that other cultures have just as much to give as ours. She taught me that people from all around the world are fascinating and full of customs and wisdom to give me and that I must learn to forgive even those who have done the worst to me because life is short and the arts are about love. I will try to follow in her footsteps and keep making things and helping people until I'm in my nineties. She was my real mother. She will always be my mama. She gave me a wonderful life.

January 17, 2011

Stretching Boundaries: The Merlin of La Mama (1986)

For those who know La Mama and its guardian spirit, Ellen Stewart, the theater represents a haven for experimentation, wild triumphs and terrifying mistakes. For those who've never heard of the place, I like to explain La Mama as the Marx Brothers version of the United Nations, where Tibetan monks are encouraged to learn to belly dance and American playwrights are bullied to abandon their fraught obsessions with Western narcissism. At La Mama we learn to move our rib cages in five different directions, chant three pitches at the same time, and make masks out of wet mud. La Mama is, and has been for a quarter century, passionately dedicated to global exchange.

Ellen Stewart is, in this daughter's eye, a kind of quixotic Wonder Woman, who has withstood several changes of political climate, artistic trendiness and cynical attacks. For those of us who come and go—to Broadway, Hollywood, to European opera, the rock 'n' roll concert stage—she remains fixed in her Merlin-like cave on Fourth Street, and when we return from "just those things you have to do, baby," she is never resentful, always delighted to see us, and has a "Korean classical opera singer honey in the Korean style, you've just got to hear, she dances too; but those high notes honey those high notes."

This is the twenty-fifth anniversary of the La Mama Experimental Theater. In those twenty-five years, the diversity of the La Mama population has grown to staggering proportions, reflecting Ellen's nurturing self. Also, La Mama's spaces, particularly the Annex, attract artists who don't want to be trapped in a conventional proscenium.

Over the years, La Mama has housed the plays of Sam Shepard, Tom Eyen, Lanford Wilson, Jean-Claude van Itallie, Harold Pinter, Paul Foster, Megan Terry, Ed Bullins, Rochelle Owens, Terence McNally, and so many others whose work needed space, funding and minimal interference. Creator-directors such as Wilford Leach, Joe Chaikin, Tom O'Horgan, Marshall Mason, Andrei Serban, Meredith Monk, Ping Chong and the Mabou Mines founded the beginnings of strong repertories and continuity. Peter Brook chose the Annex for the American premiere of *The Conference of the Birds*.

Troupes from all over Europe, Eastern Europe and Scandinavia have always wanted to come to La Mama as an honor. Third world repertories are performed under the auspices of the growing La Mama Third World Institute for Theater Arts Studies (TWITAS). The Pan Asian Repertory found its home at La Mama. Bette Midler, Diane Lane, F. Murray Abraham, Philip Glass, the late Bill Elliot, Estelle Getty and many other famous names add on to a long list of all kinds of people known and unknown who along with Ellen Stewart have tried to stretch the boundaries of theater.

Ellen would give a literal-minded anthropologist the shakes. Her cultural knowledge is not book-learned, but comes from years and years of complicated travel. To watch her book a plane ticket is to watch a genius mathematician piecing together a lengthy proof. Ellen may need to go to Nairobi but if she decides to stop in Finland, Caracas and Seoul on the way, she'll plan her flights so not a moment or penny is wasted. Often she does this for austerity, but now I think she's just a junkie for obscure charter airlines.

Every place she stops she finds music and theater, meets entrepreneurs, and dreamers. She takes down names on scraps of paper, and I love to peek over her shoulder and catch the area code for the likes of a public phone outside a schoolhouse in Mali or the number for the uncle of a girl who plays the nose flute in Crete. To Ellen Stewart, all people are truly equal. Every person has the potential to do something, and that "something," whether it's menial or poetic, has had ardent support. This is rare. Generosity is gone from many institutions. La Mama is full of Ellen's adopted souls. It's symphonic in its layers and themes, and it moves fast. Ellen keeps going. Ellen is the most musical individual I know. Her range and interest is detailed and opinionated. She has the kind of delicate ear which "needs" a finger cymbal to complete a musical hunch. Her musical hunger also insists upon low Japanese ceremonial drums, deep water drums from her native American Indians, bowed gongs, clackers from the Amazon. She knows about the holiest metal tubes of the Pygmies. (She also loves to imitate how they squat-walk and whistle their airy laugh.) She once phoned me from overseas to ask whether or not I wanted her to hire a certain Australian didgeridoo expert from the bush. She'd heard him and was "absolutely" sure he was what I needed for my oratorio *Jerusalem*.

Ellen understands a real musician because she knows the truest music speaks for real needs and real events. Rarely can unmotivated, "entertaining" music compare to that which is played to celebrate a birth, death, intense love. Motivation must come from genuine belief, connection to abstract spirit, Gods and sound. La Mama stands for the definition of musical theater which incites musicians, singers, and actors to make a real event; something that matters, an explosion that happens, as if for the first time. Music isn't "performed" in a "space" for an "audience."

Through the years, when I was working on *Trojan Women*, *Aladdin* and *Jerusalem*, Ellen would eavesdrop on my rehearsals. Sometimes, after a half-hearted day, she'd shake her head "no" or she might cover her ears. I'd get furious, and yet I knew she was right. (I've seen other artists in whom Ellen has rightfully induced a kind of artistic rabies.) She knows that only a special wakefulness and concentration can bring music to life.

Ellen Stewart's understanding of her "babies" has always been deep. She prescribes countries for the doldrums and makes sure an artist can get to the desert or ancient chapel she thinks will help him or her grow. She matches composers, actors and dancers with directors, designers and choreographers from halfway across the globe. Nothing stops Ellen when she senses a fitting combination. She materializes her plane tickets the way magicians bring out white doves. "Baby—you want to go to hear the Pygmies? You're going to the Ituri forest. Just tell me when you want to leave." "Baby I met this fantastic martial arts expert from Korea. Baby there were these people here from Italy. They think you should do your theater piece in their opera house." "Baby we gotta do Oedipus outside in an amphitheater. Delphi, honey, that's where the Oracle was. There's this group of fantastic Greeks. So nice and serious—and they can sing too." Ellen wins connections and trust worldwide because her interest in building an international symphony is genuine. Her joyous audacity is often welcome in timid communities.

At first—I was nineteen years old at the time—I thought Ellen was sabotaging my career as a folk/protest singer by taking me on a tour with Andrei Serban's company all around Europe. Then, in Paris when I saw her huddled in a corner with Peter Brook ("Mr. Peter Brook," she called him), I was sure she was trying to sell me. When "Mr. Brook" asked me into his troupe, she hugged me and said, "I think she will hear the sounds she always heard in her head but never out loud. And then Miss Swados will someday have to go to India and Persia, and Japan. Oh there are so many sounds Miss Swados has heard in her head that she doesn't know are being played by little biddies just like herself somewhere else. And when she hears that music and meets those people—oh, will we hear things from Miss Swados that we can't even imagine today." That year, of course, turned out to be one of the major influences over my creative life.

How rare is the generosity of the La Mama spirit. Ellen wants artists to meet each other not just for adventure, but because she truly believes that each artist can benefit by understanding other cultures, that art itself will grow through exchange and international collaboration. She strives to nurture those whom she believes can create an international theatrical language. She is respectful of purists, but believes that even the holiest of third-world ritual music and dance will be nothing more than museum pieces without the shock of Western energy. She thinks Western artists have everything to learn from the simplicity, commitment and visceral connection to gods of third-world "primitive" chant, mask, dance and melody. She doesn't see herself as an entrepreneur so she doesn't match chic international superstars. She's not a maker of self-proclaimed avant-garde shows or highly publicized sentimental, political events. She's messier than all that. I say this uncritically. She creates an international theatrical vision in much the same way as Charles Ives saw America. She loves the variety, holiness and filth of Egyptian shrines, Syrian and African markets; the warm, elegant stones of Spoleto.

It doesn't always matter to her whether "children" she discovers end up making classic masterpieces. I doubt that the rights to La Mama will ever be bought up to make a television series like *Fame*. Her world theater has evolved over a long stretch of uneven seasons. The individuals she's nurtured and often carried for years come from every aspect of human experience. It's unimportant to her whether anyone emerges as the star of the hour. Ellen's taste is her own. In my time, I've watched hundreds of people come and go, among them Filipino playwrights and directors, Native American writers, Noh theater master craftsmen, Moroccan painters, British costumers, French storytellers, Israeli choreographer-dancers, Argentinian song writers, Lebanese producers, Italian script writers, Polish troupes, Butoh dancers, old-time tap dancers, Cypriot religious singers, Mr. Cohen from the Orchard Street Optometrists Store, gypsy children; the list goes on and on—and I can't forget the Korean director I worked with who had a deep need to make a play about rotting seaweed. He was given a full chance.

Ellen Stewart's patience and long-range perspective make her different from any other producer in the world. Because she has never pushed to make La Mama a tryout for future profitable productions, her theater has often been on the brink of financial and creative disaster. However, after twenty-five stubborn years, it's easy to see that La Mama is everywhere. Its influence shows up in many plays, concerts and performances, where time is altered, color and shape come from other worlds, and music dares not to have a "hook." Wherever communication is nonverbal; where the sound of a word is as vital as its meaning; wherever a set, costume or mask shows the slightest resemblance to the art of another nation, La Mama's history can be recognized.

The work of artists specializing in minimalism, slow motion, ensemble acting, silent slapstick, third-world jazz, drag shows, punk shows, musicals about youth, gays, shows staged like pictures, highly physical prison plays, dance pieces with acting, one person shows with monologues, combinations of painting and music, concerts and polemics, chorale celebrations with puppets and mime—all forms owe La Mama a strong gesture of gratitude. Whether she directly influenced any specific production or not, Ellen Stewart created a massive, chaotic human enterprise which suggested the possibility of other hidden cultures joining ours. Her theater taught audiences to open up. She endured insults and poverty. Her gift of possibility is what resonates and persists.

Now we celebrate a remarkable twenty-five years. I can only go back seventeen of my own when I met the person for whom I quit college and wrote operas in dead languages.

At the age of seventeen, my hair flowed to my knees, my skirts got caught underneath the heels of my sandals. I balanced a wide body twelve-string guitar, a south Indian vina and a Turkish drum as I tripped up the five flights of steps to meet my producer for the first time. I thought I was the Eleanor Roosevelt of experimental theater music. I'd decided that I was going to combine relevance (i.e. Bob Dylan's lyrics) with the power of the Balinese monkey chorus and throw in the unpredictable eeriness of the Electric Prunes with a touch of Penderecki's *Hiroshima*, Buffy St. Marie, and a nod to Harold Arlen. I was all set to lay out my plans to Ellen when she opened the door to her apartment and I saw the most exotic looking instruments I'd ever known could exist. They hung everywhere. My plans got lost. I couldn't move.

"Yes, yes," the exotic woman smiled. "Yes, yes. Go ahead little one, bang, hit—go ahead!"

I rushed around the apartment of a woman I barely knew, collecting the sounds of low Tibetan drums, Balinese gongs, gamelan pieces, African marimbas, Nepalese bells, brass bowls, Thai harmonicas, Persian bells, an antique mandolin, an Indian accordion—to this day I remember each sound.

"You think that's something," she said. "You haven't heard anything yet."

I tried to talk a bit about my theories. I tried to list everything I knew about music. There's no telling if she paid any attention to my monologue or not. Everyone understands that Ellen's motivations for her choices are instinctual and mysterious. Basically, she stared at me and nodded as if listening to a tune. She can be all eyes.

"You're going to make some sounds, honey," she said. "Some sounds. But first there's a lot in music you've got to hear. More than the music—you know?"

She began chanting some Native American syllables. Then she described a large flute "carved in the shape of a bird. That really sounds like there's a bird inside. It's not like what you've heard . . . or what you're thinking about."

Then she inspected her new "baby." I felt her eyes travel up and down the outfit. She chuckled. Ellen had spent a long time as a bathing-suit designer at Saks and had a strong sense of fashion. Therefore, she often tried, in those years, to rid me of my Bennington draperies. I stood there in silence because I was shy, and I could also hear the echo of all those new unbelievable instruments.

"Pick up your head, baby," said Ellen. "You aren't gonna see anything staring at your feet."

I stared at all the paintings, hangings, pottery, statues, rugs and masks. Out of the corner of my eye I took in the bright stare and wide smile of my beautiful, intense new boss.

"You think that's something," she said. "You haven't seen anything yet."

II. The Story of a Street Person

The Story of a Street Person (1991)

When I was four, my brother decided to teach me manners. He claimed to know Emily Post personally, and he wanted to pass down to me the "L. J. Swados Interpretation" of her dos and don'ts. Lincoln was eleven, and I believed he was a scholar. The lesson was strict, and he didn't laugh.

"The question is: Do you want to be a lady or a pig?" he said, glaring at me through his thick fifties'-style glasses. "Pigs can't find husbands with summer cottages on Lake Erie, where brothers can come visit and go water-skiing." I tried to buckle down. First, I learned to sip my tomato soup soundlessly. This was hard, since Lincoln didn't want me to move the spoon. When I was nearly done, he told me to drink the remaining soup from the opposite end of the bowl. This required that I lean over the bowl, tip it away from me and lap at the soup with my tongue. My brother watched this maneuver carefully. Soup dribbled onto the tablecloth or down my chin. The ends of my long red hair dipped into the bowl. "You're really vying to become a spinster, you know that?" he said sadly. "No real man wants a woman who is incapable of drinking her soup upside down from a real china bowl. Mommy and Daddy will be so embarrassed. You'll have to marry an insurance salesman like Uncle Irving." He dabbed tenderly at the red splotches on my chin and collar. I tried not to cry. My crying infuriated him.

"The last lesson," Lincoln said to me, "is how to act gracefully if your napkin catches fire on the candelabrum and there's no butler with a fire extinguisher nearby." He lighted all the candles on the Hanukkah menorah he'd brought out for our "formal dinner" and then set his paper napkin on fire. He watched the flames until they reached the tips of his long, grubby fingers.

"Lincoln," I cried. I was scared.

At the last moment, he shoved the burnt napkin in the crystal water glass. Sparks and smoke hissed up into the kitchen.

"Tra-la," my brother sang victoriously. "The idea is not to set your host's tablecloth or rug on fire. Now you try."

I sat quietly, staring at the fuzzy particles of the burnt napkin floating in the darkened glass.

"No," I said. "Mommy'll get mad. I'm scared."

"We're talking about Emily Post. I'm trying to teach you to become a lady."

Even at four, I knew that burning a napkin on a menorah had nothing to do with finding a rich husband.

"No," I whined.

"Stop whining!" my brother growled at me. "Whining, you little brat, can put you in the penitentiary of whiners. No one ever leaves there; they just whine themselves to death."

He stood up, knocking over his chair as he did so, stalked to his room and slammed the door. Soon I heard strains of Frank Sinatra coming from his record player. Lincoln sang along, as he often did when he was comforting himself. He was out of tune, but he'd memorized the phrasing perfectly. Our live-in maid, Marie, returned from shopping and swiftly cleaned up the mess and me before my parents returned for dinner. I was ashamed at having let my brother down. Winning his forgiveness was a long and complicated task. I seemed destined to be the focus of his love, expectations and experiments. I was also the one who constantly betrayed the very core of his hope.

Lincoln lived in filth from a young age. He started smoking early, and cigarette butts made crusty mountains in his ashtrays. As early as eighth grade, he began writing prolifically, and his papers were stuffed in sock drawers and shoved under dressers. The India ink from his drawings spilled into multicolored stains. He'd begun what would be a lifelong passion for collecting symbolic objects. Broken toys, half-cracked clocks, strings and keys were hidden in corners of his closet, the floor of which overflowed with dirty clothes.

I know all this because I sneaked into Lincoln's room whenever he was out. I thought he was a genius, and I wanted to read every word he had written. I believed it might be catching—that I'd gain wisdom, maturity or religious enlightenment by glancing at an unfinished cartoon or mouthing the words of one of his poems.

Years later, when I crawled through the smashed windows of his

Lower East Side storefront to recover any papers or objects that might be too private to fall into the hands of the press or scavengers, I was struck with horror at how Lincoln's world looked like the stinking hovel of a madman. The objects seemed random, rusty. Cat food and litter covered everything. The papers were yellowed scraps. They had become incoherent notes scribbled on torn paper. I thought about how schizophrenia was a degenerative disease and how Lincoln had fought the chaotic choruses, movies and soundtracks in his brain to hold on to the moments of clarity that were allotted him. From an early age, he'd spend whole days in bed, exhausted from his battles. He was pasty-faced, thin, with bloody gums and lingering colds. He had many small infections, from hangnails to conjunctivitis. His eyesight grew worse and worse. I've been told by several doctors and psychologists that the life expectancy of a severe schizophrenic is shorter than that of a so-called normal person. I never listened. And I never expected my brother to die young. No one told me he was diagnosed as schizophrenic until I was in my twenties.

The principal of Lincoln's private school in Buffalo called up my parents and told them that he, the dean and the school psychologist were recommending that Lincoln attend a special institutional school, where he would receive strong discipline and therapy. A dismal anxious mood settled into the household. Lincoln kept entirely to his room. My mother went to bed. My father's voice boomed down our hallways as he talked to specialists on the phone.

Some of the accusations against Lincoln were: He had a terrible problem with authority. He drew obscenities on the walls. He recited nonsensical poems, interrupting other students and causing chaos in the classroom. He handed in copies of famous short stories instead of assignments. He had sodomized several boys in the locker room. He ran naked through chapel. He sold marijuana at lunch. I have no idea if any of these stories was true. If I ask my family about Lincoln as a boy, they say he was "difficult but extremely charming—talented, brilliant, but a little wacky." No one could face what they didn't dare to see.

My father removed Lincoln from the claustrophobic private school and put him into Riverside High School, the giant public high school with students of all backgrounds from our entire zoning district. Lincoln seemed to flourish. He gave me cheerleaders' pompons, and said he'd been "commissioned" to write cheers for the football team. He joined the drama club. When the family took a vacation to New York, he rhapsodized over our visit to my uncle, a well-known set designer, and his glamorous wife, a cosmetics executive. Lincoln said he would be a rich artist, too, with an apartment in Greenwich Village and hundreds of famous smart friends who were poets, painters and musicians. He said I could live there with him and be his maid.

When we traveled to Florida, he dressed up every night for dinner. I remember his shiny crew cut, blue seersucker jacket and white bucks. I remember the night he won the mambo contest at the Fontainebleau. I think we all drank from the prize bottle of champagne and Lincoln got drunk. He insisted on sharing his prize with the master of ceremonies and the maitre d'. My father became extremely uncomfortable with the two hotel employees sitting at our table and complimenting our family. Lincoln, however, was high as a kite and wanted to thank the strangers for "giving the youth of America a chance."

He never made it through his freshman year at Syracuse. In the beginning, he was happy. He wrote stories, poems, acted in plays and published cartoons in the college newspaper. But Lincoln had trouble registering for classes. And once he'd finally registered, the class work overwhelmed him. He simply didn't study. I remember a tense visit my parents and I made that autumn. My father was concerned about letters he'd been receiving from the dean of students. My mother was horrified at the condition of Lincoln's room. (There was half a pizza stuck to the ceiling.) Lincoln looked pasty and thin. He confided to me that he was writing a novel and had time for nothing else. My parents' mood was dark and quiet, and I knew we had to get out before there was a blowup.

Lincoln promised to write, but he never did. Several months later, my father received an almost book-length letter from my brother describing himself as in a helplessly disoriented state. He was unable to go to classes, unable to leave his room. The voices in his head were directing him to do too many different things. My father showed the letter to several psychiatrists, who recommended that Lincoln be hospitalized immediately. My father picked up Lincoln from college and committed him to a private institution.

My brother went to college and never returned. He didn't come home for Thanksgiving. He didn't bring me Hanukkah presents, and he didn't attend my grammar-school graduation. I was depressed most of the time. My only recourse was an old rusty guitar I'd borrowed from my cousin. I strummed and picked it hours a day. I learned all of Peter, Paul & Mary, Phil Ochs, Tom Rush, Joan Baez, Dave Van Ronk and Joni Mitchell. I began to write songs, ballads full of longing and confusion. Every one of them was for my brother. My parents told me he'd decided to take time off and live in New York.

My family didn't intend to create a damaging situation by lying to me. It was just that there was no precedent. They didn't know what to do. Mental illness at that time constituted the shame of shames. My father couldn't accept that Lincoln's sickness was not an act of will on the part of a severely delinquent boy. Schizophrenia is an extremely guilt-provoking disease. It often strikes promising, gentle, bright young people, and the rapid changes into incoherency and vicious rejection are almost impossible to understand. The acceptance that it is a disease is the only positive first step, and my parents, disgusted, terrified and prejudiced about mental illness, couldn't even get that far.

They couldn't tell me the truth about my brother: They were protecting the younger child. Lincoln wasn't talked about in front of me. His letters were hidden. I was watched carefully for any signs of "it" myself. The sounds behind parents' closed doors can tell a child a lot. Too many nights I heard my mother's raw weeping and my father's soaring fury. The strain in their marriage was tangible. Each resorted to blaming the other for Lincoln's psychotic break. My parents were afraid of their son. He had become a monster to them.

Since Lincoln rarely came home, the next three years were filled with phone calls. I didn't know where he was calling from, but often we'd be cut off by a pay-phone operator. Sometimes he called using made-up voices. I can remember talking to a Marine sergeant from Texas, a rock 'n' roll star from England and a dying female ex-math teacher from the Midwest. Sometimes I left the phone off the hook when I went to sleep, so I wouldn't be awakened at two or three A.M.

The summer I was sixteen and Lincoln was twenty-four, I was a counselor-in-training at Camp Deer Run in Sugar Grove, PA. My job entailed being assistant to the drama counselor, musician for vespers and campfires, as well as editor of the camp newspaper, aptly titled *The Bucke and Doe*. It was an exciting, happy summer for me.

One afternoon, I was unexpectedly summoned from lunch and found my cousin and her husband waiting for me in the parking lot. We took a long walk. They told me, with great discomfort, that my brother had been hit by a truck. His right arm and leg had been amputated, and he'd been in a coma for ten days. My parents were with my brother in New York, and no, I couldn't visit him, because they weren't sure he was going to live. My cousins said my parents thought it would be better if I stayed at camp.

I kept wondering what kind of truck would run over my brother in New York City. A Mack Truck? A cement mixer? A pickup truck? A van? I asked my cousins. They didn't know any of the details. I cried a bit, actually for their benefit. (I was numb.) They took me to the infirmary, and the nurse, with a solemn face, gave me a large green transparent pill. I fell asleep wondering what had really happened and when—or if—I'd ever find out.

My parents spent much of that year tending to Lincoln's needs, and when they returned from New York, the rift between them grew deep. My mother was drinking, and my father stayed at his office, only to return in a foul temper. I never experienced a day without feeling the walls vibrate from his screams.

From what I understood, Lincoln was not doing well. Although he'd charmed all the nurses by waking from his coma and launching into a medley of Rodgers and Hammerstein songs, he wasn't facing the reality of the arduous work that lay ahead. He'd been transferred to the Rusk Institute, one of the best clinics in the country. Lincoln could not, or would not, learn to walk on the prosthesis that was made for his leg, and refused to have a crucial operation on his shoulder so he could be fitted for a metal hand. He became so nasty, outrageous and uncooperative that he was thrown out of Rusk.

One day, I got the courage to ask my father what had really happened to my brother. He examined me with his large eyes and, after a long pause, he seemed to decide that I could take the impact of what he was about to say.

"It seems that Lincoln tried to kill himself. He jumped in front of a subway train."

When I was allowed to visit him several months later, Lincoln wanted me to believe he lived alone. The Upper East Side apartment where I met him didn't fool me. The tiny one-bedroom had none of his clutter or smell. Another name was on the buzzer and mailbox. I guessed he was back at the clinic, but I played along.

He also wanted me to be very aware that he had stumps. He greeted me in boxer shorts. I was so terrified of doing the wrong thing, and so numbed by what I saw, that I couldn't possibly register any disgust. I just said: "They're not so bad. They're kind of sexy." My brother, who had scars from head to toe, hugged me with relief. He showed me the cartoons he'd been drawing with his left hand, and although his lines were a bit shaky, the characters were wonderful. Lincoln seemed clearheaded and cheerful. I spent my whole visit praising him. He hopped around the tiny apartment singing verses from songs he was writing. He planned a club act with an elderly female pianist. He wanted to perform at the Café Wha.

Lincoln could hardly walk on his prosthesis, but he insisted on taking me out for Chinese food. When we crossed Third Avenue, all the cars and taxicabs had to stop. I asked myself: Do I stay with him or run ahead? What would insult him? What does he want? The honking and screaming was terrible, and by the time we reached the restaurant neither of us was very hungry. Lincoln was exhausted. I saw that he was heavily medicated. He asked me to hail a cab and take him to the clinic. In the cab, I put my hand over his and just let it lie there. He made small clicking sounds in his mouth. When we reached the clinic, he pecked me on the cheek and told me not to come in. I had the cab drive me around Central Park several times, so the visit would seem longer to my parents, who were waiting for me at the Westbury Hotel.

The next time I saw my brother was approximately two years later, when both of us ended up living on the Lower East Side. I was sleeping on the third floor of the La Mama theater, and Lincoln had found a storefront down the block at 99 East Fourth Street, between Second and First Avenues. He was working at the La Mama box office. Lincoln was determined to become a writer, having just spent a term at the Columbia University writing school, and I had dropped out of Bennington to try my hand at composing music for experimental theater. Lincoln and I barely spoke. He and I both believed that in the realm of "artistic truth" he was the real talent in the family and I was a dilettante playing around.

New York City streets are dangerous. The Lower East Side is infested with heroin users and crack dealers. Much of the population of Alphabet City (as the blocks around avenues A, B and C are called) remains desperately poor. But ominous streets were the least of Lincoln's worries. The main enemy of the untreated schizophrenic is time. The schizophrenic deteriorates. The schizophrenic must use up an inordinate amount of energy dealing with paranoid delusions and with the chaotic life style that results from being only marginally able to take care of oneself. It is the art of schizophrenia to sabotage any positive gestures of help.

Lincoln showed many of these characteristics. Often he spent most of his allowance before it came time to pay the rent. He'd ask me for names of people in the music business, and just as I'd be compiling a list, I'd receive a diatribe blaming me for old wounds, ordering me to forget his last request. He launched into a lengthy, incoherent monologue about Jesus at a large, extremely observant Seder. Those who romanticize madness might regard this kind of behavior as the rebellious, symbolic acting-out of unappreciated visionaries. This is too idealistic a take on the subject. The schizophrenic is a perfect machine of self-destruction. The body and the mind wear down from fighting voices, living in filth, maneuvering the streets. Despite all this, Lincoln still managed to get out of his foam-rubber bed each day, drag himself to the street (sometimes he traveled by skateboard) and play the harmonica for his neighborhood audience.

One day I was walking home from the Public Theater, and I

32

recognized my brother's slow, patient gait headed toward me. It was pouring and I had an umbrella, but he'd covered himself by stuffing his hat with newspapers. Instinct told me I didn't have to cross the street and avoid him. I walked straight ahead. He was lively, awake and happy.

"Give us a kiss," he said.

We hugged. His filthy parka was soaked.

"Isn't this rain terrific?" he said. "It cleans everything."

I offered him my umbrella.

"No, no," he laughed. "I've got my visor." (He pointed to the newspapers.) "I've got my tap shoes." His long hair dripped water and his broken glasses were steamed.

We said goodbye and he launched into an out-of-tune version of "Singin' in the Rain."

At one point, Lincoln broke his hip. At first, he didn't know what had happened to him. Family and friends, as usual, had different versions. One cousin said he'd fallen off a chair while changing a light bulb. Someone else said he'd gotten into trouble in Miami and had been pushed in front of a car. Someone else said he'd stepped in front of the car. No one could get Lincoln to leave his bed. I talked to him on the phone.

"I hurt," he said. "I really hurt. I think I hurt my shoulder."

He sounded tearful and scared, like a small boy.

"Do you want me to come and visit you?" I asked.

"Don't even try—I won't let you in," was his reply.

Finally, through the efforts of some cousins and a social worker, he was taken to Mount Sinai, where the hip fracture was detected. Surgery was required, and he was confined to a wheelchair for at least two months. Lincoln returned from the hospital and occupied his storefront with a large Hispanic male helper. He didn't go outside for a long time. I went to Israel to conduct, and had a miserable experience. For the first time in my life, I couldn't concentrate. I became obsessed with my brother's health. I was tearful and anxious. I knew he was on the verge of a rapid decline.

About that time, Lincoln was informed that his building was going co-op and that he'd have to move out of his storefront. The Lower

East Side was changing, and had been for several years. People call it gentrification, but it wasn't just the new co-ops all around that startled me. It was the change in population. Now, tourists came on weekends to browse in the new boutiques and eat in the wood-paneled restaurants. Prices rose astronomically, and "freaks" were just another attraction for uptown visitors to gape at. Second Avenue and its surroundings were prime real estate. My brother was an innocent victim in a cycle of change. His beloved neighborhood was turning on him.

He was walking again, but he'd done little to deal with his landlord's notice. I found a lawyer who managed to negotiate a deal in which Lincoln would get $25,000 from the landlord for his storefront. He seemed pleased. He told everyone that he was going to use the money to go to Miami, where he could street-sing all year round. He had friends there, he said. Did anyone ask him where he would live? I don't know.

Lincoln had been perhaps the greatest influence over my childhood, and he still continued to live inside my head. I sensed that he'd never endure leaving his home of fifteen years. It was like a beaver's dam stocked full of his memorabilia. The walls were constructed from the trash that constituted his sacred objects. He knew everyone in the vicinity. He knew how many steps it took to get to his restaurants and stores. If he moved one block away, the rituals of his life would be shattered.

By the time I began searching the East Side for first-floor apartments he'd be able to afford, I think the crisis was past undoing. Also, I had no idea how expensive rents had become. Even with my help, there was almost no affordable space for Lincoln to move into that would be near his beloved territory. My cousin had secured him a place at Fountain House, a halfway house with a rehabilitation program, but at first Lincoln refused to consider it, and when he finally agreed to go for an interview, he didn't show up. A friend found him a room uptown at the Y, but Lincoln said he had no money. The date for his eviction was closing in on him, and Lincoln had managed to create a scenario wherein he had absolutely no place to go.

Most middle-class people are haunted by the homeless, the so-called Bowery bums and crazy people who populate the streets of New York.

We all get panhandled. We often walk past ragged creatures who sleep on gratings and whose urine trails into the street. The middle-class person asks: "How did these people get here? Who are they? Where are their families? How did they fall so low?" We all harbor fears about the difference between the mad street people and ourselves. How far are we from losing all our money and our grace and ending up ranting on a corner, holding up a piece of cardboard over a cup?

Some people romanticize the plight of the homeless as if each life were the content of a folk song. Others point to Reagan and maintain that he broke the back of the poor in our country. Still others understand enough to see that some people are on the streets because of cutbacks during the Koch Administration and the resulting lack of hospitalization, care and housing for the mentally ill. But generalizations are worthless. Every person has a different story. Each one of them was brought low by a specific, personal demon. When you think this way, the conditions in the street become unbearable. You are in touch with the individual humanity of homeless people and can't block out their suffering by blaming a "global condition."

Several months before my brother's housing crisis reached its peak, I was walking down Broadway on my way to a Korean deli. I saw two derelicts seated in the middle of the sidewalk. They were dressed in layers of rags and having a heated argument about Jesus Christ. One of them had paraphernalia spread around him in a semicircle, as if to sell his wares. But none of his rags or rusty pieces of metal or torn papers was a recognizable item. He wore a jaunty cap pulled to one side, and there was tinsel in his filthy hair. His face was smeared black. A few steps farther along, I realized the "derelict" was my brother. I leaned down next to him, softly said his name and waited. He stared at me for several moments and didn't recognize me at first. When he finally saw that it was me, he let out a cry like a man who'd had a stroke and couldn't express his joyous thoughts. We embraced for a long, long time. His smell meant nothing to me.

"We're just sitting here today," Lincoln said. "Oh, what a perfect day."

"I'm so glad to see you," I said.

"Yes," my brother replied. "You look beautiful. We get a big audience from Tower, but of course you know that, you know all that, and besides, my music requires a different audience."

I didn't want him to go off in an angry direction.

"I like your hat," I said.

He grinned. The rotten brown condition of his teeth made me wince.

"You like it? It was a gift from my friend Ann."

"I love it," I said.

"We'll be doing a lot of playing today," said my brother. "The band decided to try a new location. It's very important."

"I'd like to hear it," I said.

He frowned.

"It won't be for a while," he said.

I hugged him again, and he rocked me back and forth.

"Now this is good and enough," he said.

I let go of him, turned around and went home. I lay down on my bed and slept for fourteen hours.

Ellen Stewart, the founder of La Mama, called and told me about the shed the landlords had built in front of the building where Lincoln lived. He was two weeks late in vacating his storefront, according to the agreement, and they wanted to begin construction.

"He's barricaded in there," she told me. "I've gone down and knocked on the wood, but I can't get in."

I ran down to his block and saw what had been described to me. A large wooden shed had been erected that blocked off all the storefronts. The shed had no windows. The one door was at the opposite end from Lincoln's apartment. I tried it several times; it was locked. I tried to figure out where Lincoln's door would be in relation to the wood in front of it, and I banged my fists on the wood over and over again.

"Lincoln," I said. "This is your sister. Let me take you out of there."

Silence. I didn't know if he couldn't hear me or wouldn't hear me. It was eerie.

I tried entering the shed for a few more days. Some people thought Lincoln had moved out. No one had seen him. Finally, on February 23, I called the lawyer who had negotiated the settlement for him and told her I was on my way to the police station. Just as I was leaving, she called me back.

"Lincoln is dead," she told me. "The landlord let himself in with a key and found him. He just called." I dashed down to 99 East Fourth Street and saw the police car and the coroner's car. Several policemen were standing in the doorway. They didn't believe I was his sister. In a fury, I took out an American Express card to prove my name.

His small storefront was cluttered, and he was lying on the floor. The coroner wouldn't let me go near him.

"Why?" I asked. "Why can't I be near him?"

Someone escorted me out. It seemed ironic that I was never going to be allowed to spend time with my brother. In life or in death. His rules still held.

My father wanted nothing to do with Lincoln's death, so I was in charge of the details. I arranged for his cremation at a Second Avenue mortuary. I went to the coroner's office and identified the body. Although there is still no clear conclusion as to what caused my brother's death, his autopsy showed that, at the age of forty-six, he had blockage in his bowels and intestines, a tumor on his lung, emphysema and arteriosclerosis, which was very advanced for his age. He'd been dead several days, so they showed me a snapshot. His face was a terrifying purple-red, as if he'd been brutally beaten or burned. The bite of his mouth had rearranged itself. He looked ferocious and devilish. I thought, "He looks like a werewolf."

I worked hard to please Lincoln with the memorial ceremony. We held it at La Mama. There was a harmonica player and a Hispanic Catholic priest. Ellen Stewart spoke. A rabbi flew in from Buffalo to accompany my father. He said Kaddish. Several of my friends sang and played shakuhachis—Japanese flutes. I wasn't prepared for the flood of people who filled the small theater. I didn't realize Lincoln had so many friends and such a community of admirers.

I've said goodbye to Lincoln many times, and haven't yet successfully lost him. His voice still whispers in my head. The image of his angry face looms in front of me like the ominous head of the Wizard of Oz. "Manners are everything," he says. "You violate me, and you'll never go to a dinner party as long as you live." I stay awake at night wondering whether I should try to publish his lively collection of cartoons. I can't figure out if he'd be happy, or if I'd break some code of honor I know nothing about. The darkness of my room becomes too busy. I decide to have one small lamp burning near my closet, where Lincoln could be hiding, ready to spring.

III. Work

Listening Out Loud, "The Opening" (1989)

As a small child I lived near a zoo, surrounded by the sounds of animals and birds. Some of these sounds frightened me: the lion's roar, the bleat of a seal, and especially the blaring trumpet of the elephant. When I was five, I began to count the elephant's blasts and the spaces that existed between them, to notice other sounds that entered those spaces, how long they lasted, how frequently they occurred. Discerning a pattern in the zoo voices, organizing a kind of animal symphony in my mind, put me in control of the sounds and made me less frightened. I also got to know the sounds very well in the process. I re-created them as best I could by imitating with my voice while plucking on a clothesline or hitting an empty pot.

Around that time, I began studying classical piano and was required to practice each day. While I pretended I was playing assigned pieces, I began to spend the time improvising. When the practice hour was over, I would remain at the piano to write songs.

Once again I lost myself in sounds. I explored the difference between pounding a furious chord and touching a single note; the blur of the soft pedal, which seemed to ring the noted on forever; and the zip of three notes played as fast as my fingers could go. When I found a pattern I liked, I repeated it. The power of the sounds grew as I came to understand better how I made them. My songs got longer as I added tiny new sections onto each memorized discovery. I didn't, at that time, think about an audience any more than I'd fantasized about applause for my giant zoo orchestra. I'd found a language that was secret, controllable, and my own. My senses woke up; I sweated as if I were doing sports; I felt brave and excited as if I were a heroine at the beginning of a long adventure. At the age of five, I didn't care about the other composers whose music sat on the piano. The idea that anyone might know my sounds would have seemed absurd. No one else had been there. No one heard what I heard. I owned the world.

Over the years I've learned to speak the language of those who experience the world through their eyes, rather than ears. I can pass by a diner on the road and think about Edward Hopper. I'm aware of the formations of geese when they take off. I enjoy sports, dances, and parks and take great pleasure from the walking styles and mannerisms of my fellow human beings. Left to my own devices, however, I hardly see the diner. I hear the crash and clank of the dishes juxtaposed against Bruce Springsteen blaring over a jukebox while a radio sportscaster shouts scores. I laugh at the geese, whose flapping and calls sound like bicycle horns in a Marx Brothers routine. And professors, street characters, friends, and lovers often remain as voices in unwritten operas and songs. I measure their louds and softs, the patterns of their speech and steps. I'm fascinated by how emotions cause pitch to soar, strain, or drop. Perhaps, in this way, I distance myself from the verbal interactions of day-to-day life. I see the potential of underscoring each confrontation or attraction. Song cues come to me during crucial decisions. Sound is the medium through which I perceive life. A composer uses sound to try to shape, understand, and express her daily pleasures and her unanswered questions.

The passion for organizing sounds and the desire to own and shape them are characteristic of all composers. And I think it's likely that most of them experience these drives early in life. An extraordinary relationship to sound and a fanaticism about it are not skills that one makes a conscious decision to develop. They are givens for the composer, to whom an event is a complex opera of sound that he or she desires not to act in or tell about but to govern as an absolute ruler, wielding instruments, harmonies, rhythms.

Stirred by a sound that originates in the mind or in the outside world, the composer seeks to possess that sound, to capture the experience of it. Let's say, for example, I hear outside my window an old man walking in the street, humming a Yiddish melody in a scratchy voice. Perhaps I can catch the essence of this with a violin, making it somewhat squeaky, the rhythm uneven, the voicing slightly off-key. The sound should have a haunting quality and an uneven absentmindedness.

Perhaps I hear longing in his voice. I imagine a village near an ancestor's town in Latvia. I hear his mother singing him the tune. He sings it thinking of her, of the loss of her, of the loss of that town and that time. He's uncomfortable on the sidewalk, in the heat, lonely, not sick but short of breath. He's not bitter, but he needs an old tune to push the bad thoughts from his head during his daily walk. Has the old man's humming contained all of these elements? Probably not. In the process of translating my experience of his sound, I have supplied them. His music becomes mine now.

The art of taking something from instinct and accident and making it permanent is what composing is all about. And when a composer can retain a sound's original freshness and power even while transforming it, she has succeeded.

A talented listener can distinguish my intentions in the Yiddish melody. Such a listener might identify with the emotional background and perhaps even analyze the technical choices that brought about the expression of longing, unevenness, fatigue, and sweetness. A gifted performer would try to fulfill my wishes by finding the exact position of the bow to produce a strong scratchiness; a full stroke to invoke the old melody, a position above the bridge to make breathlessness. But neither the listener nor the performer possesses the need to transform an old man's humming into a repeated, permanent form. The performer needs to play with it. The listener is nourished by some identification with its mood. The composer is propelled to make a moving structure of sounds, whether inspired by a chance encounter or passionate idea. Gifted listeners find satisfaction in reinterpreting the intention of the composition while it's being performed. Performers dig deeply into the composer's ideas and, with their own instincts and intelligence, bring her hidden intentions to the world. A composer, answering to no one, works alone, sorting through sounds, structures, and dreams.

Thus she is able, almost instantaneously, to analyze the fragments, the little cells, within a sound, whether it comes from an instrument, a building being torn down across the street, or a purely internal source. She knows what is percussive about the sound, what is legato, what is melodic. She also knows its pitch, its duration, whether it goes up or down, how long it resonates.

Similarly, a composer must have an acute understanding of time. Time in music is literal; it is written out. It gives the music its pulse, its beat. What effect is produced if the beat quickens or slows down? How does one intensify in the midst of a piece? What about hesitations, a syncopation? How long should it take to develop a theme?

In my opera *Lullabye and Goodnight*, I made a duet from the progression of an argument between a tough prostitute and her pimp. She's holding money back and he coaxes, cajoles, abuses, terrorizes. I can't take an hour to make it come to a violent climax as it might in real life. I must condense the progression into a four- or five-minute duet. I begin by having the pimp's voice dominate the dialogue. He carries the downbeats, the heavy accents. He's berating, threatening. The prostitute coyly responds in syncopated leading lines, fitted in between the pimp's accusations. Because my character is a fighter, her responses to the pimp's badgering begin to grow in length as they do in power. I divide the measures more equally. The pimp sings for four measures. Their voices become a battle of syncopated drumbeats. My "cut time" reflects the parrying of the two furious business partners. By the end of the argument, the characters are singing different rhythms at the same time, both filling equal space, working against each other's rhythms as well as gaining momentum by the differences in inflection, consonants, and vowels. In good composing, words and music are treated as joined forces for energetic sound. The mutual hesitations, duplicities, flirtations, exhausted entreaties, and rages have been translated into musical time.

Different composers might use time differently in this situation. A more naturalistic composer may expand the argument to a twenty-minute operatic scene with interventions from street noises and outside characters. A popular songwriter might find a single point of view and rap it in a two-minute talking blues. An avant-garde serial composer might being scattered phrases related to the argument in and out of a more abstracted, synthesized urban environment. Any composer, however, must deal with the necessity of setting the argument to fixed time, much as a painter must work within a fixed space.

Music is a nonverbal art form that appeals to our emotions rather than to out intellect. To be sure, sounds can be given a mathematical explanation: if an accent is two beats away from another, it produces a certain effect; if three beats separate the notes, the effect will be different, and so on. But that does not really explain our response. Music speaks to the unconscious.

Composers are by nature believers in magical powers. Throughout the history of religion and mythology, sound has been endowed with the power to produce supernatural results. Aladdin conjures the genie and opens the gate by uttering a sound. The mantric word "om" in Indian religion is believed to clear the system of outside energies that disperse concentration and cause dark moods and laziness of the soul. The sounds itself is a kind of spiritual vacuum cleaner. Egyptian lore maintains that one can levitate by chanting certain notes while sitting in the middle of a pyramid. The Hopi Indians have chants and songs that cause creatures to come bearing wisdom from the spirits of other worlds. A lion can be stopped from killing, according to jungle mythology, by producing with the voice a sound that speaks in the direct language of the beasts. Sounds have been endowed with the power to heal, to change weather, to afford access to deity.

Early music was prayer. Incantation is at the root of song. The repeated one- or two-note style of Eastern singing now popular in the styles of minimalist and New Age composers has always existed. There are few cultures that don't pray and whose prayer songs don't somehow influence composers. Gregorian chant strives for simplicity and purity of tone. Its quiet ecstasy winds its way into a great deal of early European classical music, where emotion is meant to be expressed with discretion and privacy. In contrast, the davening of Jewish prayer is less contained. The voice of a cantor is often openly tearful or joyous. The love of God is sung out loud with no need for quiet. I trace the pristine, jubilant oratorios of Handel and cantatas of Bach to Gregorian chant, and I can feel the furious rhythms and sweet melodies of my forefathers' shuls behind Gershwin's and Arlen's jazz songs and even Bernstein's Italian/Latin "street music" in *West Side Story*. The child inside every good person believes that a prayer might change bad to good. A sweet prayer gives thanks for a happy event. An urgent prayer asks for guidance in an emergency. Every culture mourns its dead in song. Music is a vast archive of the nonverbal wishes that have been passed down from generation to generation.

In the late twentieth century in Western society, composers most likely do not perceive sound as possessing specific magical properties. They do not believe that sounds cause the sun to rise or the harvest to flourish. Their primary motivation is not incantation. But I think that, however conscious or unconscious, it is part of the composer's belief system that music has the power to make things happen. I wrote my oratorio *Jerusalem*, which brings together the sound of Muslims, Jews, Christians, and the many ethnic groups in Israel, because I wanted to hear those voices combined. At the same time, I believed that singing together would create harmony: the magical element that music, and only music, can produce. A composition begins with the composer's need to organize a set of sounds that is building up in the mind and demanding to get out. It is impossible not to feel a bit like a witch doctor when one gains control of this inarticulate world of sound, orders it, and makes it actually happen.

Composing, then, is both a worker's craft and a holy expression, and these seemingly contradictory elements reflect certain parts of the composer's nature. A composer is childlike in her dependence on nonverbal impulses that will make her seem immature, possessive, and moody. However, she must also be pragmatic, orderly, and objective. The composer is a construction worker, building something with notes and layers and time, taking care of what Pierre Boulez calls the "plumbing" of music.

The foundation of a musical construction is as simple as the bass line in the Temptations' song "My Girl." Other foundations are the pedal point in a Bach organ piece and the 5/8 sax bass and drum feel in Brubeck's "Take Five." The composer builds freely but carefully on her fundamentals, taking into consideration the weight, texture, and staying power of each instrumental and harmonic choice. Even when I was very young, I learned not to muddy the clarity of my sounds with top-heavy melodies that covered up my rhythms. A passion for harmony can sometimes drown out the melody it's intended to complement. Too many times I'd introduce a song to a group of friends and watch it disappear behind layers of my own ambitious orchestrations.

Knowing how to connect the phrases, to take a melodic line to an exact finish, to build an orchestration neatly into a tune, is as "nuts and bolts" as designing the pipes of one's house. The art of composition is dependent on layering, connecting, and designing workable vehicles that can move at different speeds and dynamics. If the construction is in good working order, then the composer has a chance of cutting through to touch the unconscious, causing fresh, potent feelings. It's rare that a piece of living music simply explodes from unplanned work. The exceptions happen in improvisational sessions when the players are highly skilled musicians who have learned, one way or another, the mathematical and other strict structures that give them the privilege of freedom.

In the last twenty years, many creative composers have devoted research to electronic waves—the pulse speeds and decays of synthesized sound. Composers all over the world are programming Oberheim, Roland, Yamaha, and other synthesizers to invent sounds, create samples of those sounds, and add them onto the traditional musical vocabulary. The same mathematical obsessiveness can be found in a composer who is working on a percussive wave lower than any timpani. Beethoven, who kept adding instruments and finally voices to his symphonies in order to create the biggest sound his imagination would allow, would have delighted in the synthesizer's ability to take repeated intervals and expand them, not just through variation but also by pure textural experimentation.

Composers are also very connected to rites of passage and the rituals that accompany them. They have a keen sense of event. Music has always been present during ceremonies that celebrate or eulogize. The impulse to commemorate an event, to give it a musical identity, is a strong one. In Japan, for instance, the Noh operas are connected to seasons. The Jewish Torah is read and sung according to the time of year, and composers write works based on traditional holidays. Bartok took his inspiration from Eastern European feasts and memorials. Bach and Handel connected their writings to the rituals and music of the church. As we move into contemporary music, the link with holidays becomes less obvious, but the reflection of seasons and celebration is just as evident.

Often composers write with someone specifically in mind. During freshman year at Bennington College, I lost a dear friend in a car accident. When I wrote my first orchestral piece, I wanted not only to dedicate it to her memory but to capture aspects of her for my own pleasure. She was engaged to a Hungarian, loved folk music, had a loud, raucous laugh, and liked to play the violin standing on an orange crate so her music could fly out her open window. I filled my piece with bird and wind sounds, modal riffs, and a laughing chorus. The *Kindertotenlider* was written by Mahler for the loss of a beloved child. George Crumb's *Ancient Voices of Children* was inspired by the passionate spirit of Garcia Lorca and the special quality of compassion and serenity in the voice of mezzo-soprano Jan De Gaetani.

Because of their possessive and possessed relationship to sound, composers tend to be tyrants. The way they hear sounds is the right one. Their aural vision is absolute. The result of this tendency is frequently a loss of manners. It is common for composers to be notably rude, walking out on one another's concerts, often commenting loudly as they do so. Jealousy and cruelty are not unusual in any of the arts. But in music, wicked tongues and devious behavior are common. It's an antisocial occupation. Much time is spent alone in a room with sounds. Therefore, opinions are typically expressed in grunts, boos, groans, or even more primary ways. Sometimes such reactions are intellectual—"Why did he get a Guggenheim and I didn't?"—but often they are the result of a more primitive feeling. Sounds can be physically offensive. Offensive music can cause a composer to get sick or begin on a fit of rage. My mentor went pale before my eyes after he heard what he thought was "the strains of those phony pop melodies" in one of my early operas.

Composers are clannish and tribal. They're loyal to their schools and don't forgive defection. They love strongly from the beginning; they influence one another, quote one another, feed and house one another. Then, say, an atonal serialist presents a structured melody and he's "finished;" a modernist begins to write lush chord progressions and he's a "dilettante;" a postmodernist writes a song for Linda Ronstadt and his credibility is ruined. Many great teachers demand loyalty to their singular view of what is truly modern music, what is the only true way to move forward.

I do not share this tendency toward monomania. I believe that all schools and labels have their talented and untalented artists, their share of fools and dilettantes. I try to teach that no one style of music "transcends" another, though I don't believe that entirely. I've stormed out of operas and concerts of new music. I am wary of being anyone's artistic guru. There have been years when I couldn't find a redeeming pluck in one single composition chosen for a grant or prize. The question "Why not me?" or 'Why not anyone I can respect?" is often overpowering. However, I try to control my fury and encourage my students to be attentive to new voices whether or not they are inspiring. If a composer works hard at her craft and stays true to her sound, she will become less threatened and may even develop a sense of humor about the competition.

It's difficult to stay calm when listening to one's own music being performed. I know a composer who wanted a section of his symphony to be played without any vibrato in the strings. He stood anxiously by the string section, staring at the left hands of the players as if examining each finger for the slightest waver. He made the conductor and concertmaster increasingly irritable and got himself banned from the rehearsals. He wasn't a Hollywood movie version of a mad artist. Symphonic string sections rarely play without vibrato, and this composer knew he was asking for something not only difficult but distasteful to many classically trained musicians. Yet the heart of this composer's vision lay within a straight, strained sound. The slightest compromise would deny him the realization of two years of work.

Let's say you are writing an ode to autumn, and you decide to use a cello, an alto flute, and an oboe because those strike you as providing the right tone colors, although to someone else they might conjure a funeral procession or sprightly Welsh dancing. And perhaps you begin this sound painting with a walk in the leaves; the cello takes that motif, the flute supplies the blowing wind, the oboe is a flock of geese overhead. If the cello player moves faster than the adagio you've designated, you may end up with something more appropriate to a romp than to a thoughtful walk. If the oboe player ignores your pianissimo and begins to play loudly, your geese are suddenly running amuck. A flat alto flute can blunt the air of longing that comes with your vision of fall.

The chances of hearing an effective performance of your work improve if you don't regard your players as the slaves who build the composer's monuments. When they are not taken for granted, musicians are among the human race's most admirable members. A composer shows respect for musicians by writing parts that challenge their technical skills and imagination. A good musician will work hard to convey the intention of a passage, if the passage is clearly intended to put his instrument to good use. Certain kinds of routine orchestrations can't be helped—consecutive measures of rests, pages of held notes, repeated patterns, and so forth—but even these easy tasks will be performed with precision if the whole work proves that the composer used the instrument and its player effectively. Musicians share the composers' understanding of pure sound and know the *feel* of it as well. Most of them are motivated by a love of music rather than a grandiose dream of stardom, and are, on the whole, quite selfless in their desire to serve the piece they are playing.

Although composers can be egocentric and narrow-minded, their clannish propensities typically cause them to be loving teachers and protective allies. My friends and I exchange letters, phone calls, telegrams, and mementos; we buy one another drinks at 3:00 A.M. and leave reassuring choruses on one another's tape machines. Because composing is a profession that frequently involves intense difficulties and disappointments, it fosters a caretaking instinct in those who practice it. Ferocious loyalty and a sense of brotherhood (I say this advisedly as there are so few women) are not uncommon.

Only the most self-important composer could possibly believe that what he or she is doing is absolutely new. Composers recognize themselves in one another's music. They know why someone picked a particular key, what someone is doing with a harmony or rhythm. They are not mystified about why something works. The mystery lies in how that composer had the inspiration or good fortune, even genius, to make such a choice. Wonder and awe come when a fellow composer uses the very same instruments—say a bass drum, piccolo, trombone— that we've listened to all our lives, and still manages to make us feel as though we've never heard those sounds before. Composers exult in such a moment as much as parents do when they celebrate their baby's first word.

When rock musicians listen to Stevie Wonder, they're astonished by the way he comes up with yet another winning hook, or by his multifaceted skills in performing, overdubbing, and producing. I've seen composers respond to the progressions in a Brahms chorale or to the rhythms Bartok creates in his piano concertos as if they were watching a gymnast give a ten-point performance in the Olympics.

Just as families do, composers have a sense of a unique shared language. It is as though we populate a small, obscure country. We speak in many dialects but in the same tongue. While other people may claim to understand us, only a fellow composer can truly catch all the nuances. If I were listening to a song with someone who was not a citizen of this strange country, I might say, "Listen to that. Doesn't it make you feel great?" Whereas if I were listening with a composer, I'd say, "What an incredible place to modulate; listen to how he brings in the bass; I love the part when it jumps into double time." To a classical composer I might say, "Modulating up a third at that moment, and putting in the pizzicato where the sustain was, sets up the expectation of a resolution, but there is none, and we're left hanging and that's true terror." This might sound like algebra to someone who doesn't know music. I've heard poets become rapturous about the placement of a comma or a pronoun. I can understand what they're so excited about, although I don't speak their tongue fluently.

The limitations of a composer's vocabulary, just twelve notes (in Western music), demand that she be meticulous and patient. Transforming the experience of sound into music is painstaking, and a composer must keep at it and keep at it until it exists on paper exactly as it sounds in the mind. The transformation process demands great organizational skills. No composer in the world can simply throw sounds together and expect them to result in music. He or she must gather them together and decide when they walk in, when they walk out, when they sit down, when they get up, when they are loud, when they are soft, when they speak together, when they don't. There is nothing random in this construction work.

What makes the construction vibrant and original and worth caring about is, on the one hand, something of a mystery; on the other hand, it's as simple as going into a market, picking up two tomatoes, and knowing which is fresh and which has gone soft. A fresh sound tastes good to the ear and brings with it a sense of your mind awakening. It makes you feel you're hearing something for the first time, and you want to hear it again.

When someone who is truly beautiful enters a room, you're riveted by his or her presence, whereas your eyes skid off someone making an "entrance," striving to impress, overly made-up, self-conscious. There is no question which is the genuine article. An authentic sound has an honesty and directness that compels attention. Hearing good music is a little like falling in love. You're not sure what hit you, but you suddenly feel shaky and excited and intensely alive. Superficial music may touch a listener in a superficial way, but only fresh, genuine sound truly moves the spirit.

The ability to create such sounds is surely a gift. But a wide variety of opinions exist about who is gifted and who is merely talented. For a young composer to spend time worrying about which she is is a waste of time. It is also a sneaky way of being lazy. Composers may fall silent for a time, or question whether they can withstand the perils of life in the profession, but they do not spend time wondering if they are real composers. Composing is an art form that leaves little room for self-doubt. The sounds themselves are insistent and irrefutable. You must write them as you hear them. You must write them to please yourself. And, most important, you must love the music for itself.

Composers, like all other people, sometimes resort to wishful thinking. All of us would like to hear thousands roaring when the baton falls at the end of the performance of one of our pieces. But I think that composers part with this fantasy rather early on. Someone seeking adulation or superstardom would do best to avoid composing as a way of life. This is particularly true for classical and jazz composers, whose chances of being neglected and misunderstood are the greatest. In this era, in which rock music commands wide attention and programs in concert halls are dominated by homage to the distant past, audiences are in effect warned before hearing new music, as though they were going to be exposed to a dangerous substance. If theatrical composers stray too far from what has been done in the musical theater for the last fifty years, to what has recently proved to be a box office smash, the audience is likely to disappear, and they will be out of work. Certainly today rock songwriters are the most likely to achieve visible success, but the majority of them ought to know that their work will never reach the limelight.

So you must have a love for the sounds you make that is satisfying in itself, because the chances of an audience liking it are smaller still. And even if they like it, the smallest chance of all is that they will want to hear it again. There is a long tradition in music, whether classical, jazz, or blues, of composers being ignored while they were alive and working, and being lionized when they died or fell silent. To enter this profession with the expectation of being loved and rewarded is folly.

Why, faced with such grim prospects, do composers persevere? Within every composer, however normal his or her exterior, there lives an obsessive. Music is not born of stable good-natured, well-balanced impulses, and no one can exist in a world of constant sound, have a fanatic relationship to it, and not be slightly mad. These sounds compel the composer to create music, for only music can truly satiate her craving of the spirit. It fills a need that no lover, child, material possession, or religion can satisfy. It is, in a sense, her definition of being alive. For a composer, writing music is more than a form of artistic expression. It is a way of life.

I've always been fascinated by the poets of Russia who survived long periods of political and artistic isolation and still wrote so beautifully. I am particularly moved by the life of Anna Akhmatova, who went from being a famous poet to a political pariah, to "nonentity," to impoverished old woman, to a revered voice of her people. Besides her life's dramatic struggle, I found inspiration in her constant use of the "little things" in her work. She wrote about hems of dresses, flags on holidays, tattered maps. The act of planting flowers became an event for her art. I liked her simple step-by-step way of perceiving.

It is a gift composers can apply to music. There's much to do. Every sound of pitches and rhythms brings new relationships to the ear. There's always a task of documenting and transforming experience through the private language of sounds and dreaming what the outcome will be when the music inside the head comes to life outside. Each note progresses into a pattern or melody, each sound into a set of beats or effects. There's so little time to finish all the technicalities. I know I can get lost in the terrible despair that accompanies being insulted, misunderstood, or passed over. However, I doubt that I or many other composers permanently give in to our bitterness. Too many sounds interrupt even a happy flow of thought. Decisions don't last. Sounds take over and demand immediate attention. We leave the daily life to go to our rooms and capture its reverberations through our music.

Job: He's a Clown (1994)

A couple of years ago I translated the Book of Job into a live, musical circus of clowns. But before doing so, I studied the texts and commentaries on the text. I started by reading the King James translation and was struck by the Beckett-like fairy tale feeling of the prose and the contrast of the dark end-of-the-world quality of the lamentations. Most important I spent many hours with clowns, improvising on themes that resonated in the biblical poetry. We didn't restrict our style of clowning to what might seem "respectful" to Job. We explored everything from the ridiculous Three Stooges type of slapstick to the more classical venue of mime. We excerpted small sections from the text and tried out our interpretations in front of different audiences. We didn't discriminate. We showed our work to everyone from Asian and Afro-American children to Jewish scholars. The interpretation of Job held its own, and I forged ahead to create a musical clown show.

Setting certain texts to music offered new problems. When should the music evoke liturgical sounds and when should it reflect the more popular feel of clown routines? These questions could only be answered by what was happening onstage in response to the ancient words themselves. Often the results were odd and unexpected, but quite thrilling.

After many months of work, Job *opened Off-Broadway, had a successful run, and has placed in many arenas ever since. As I look back on my notes, I'm aware that Job as a clown is not the only Job. Job as a clown is not the definitive interpretation. There was a helpless, human spirit inside of him that beckoned me, and I took the metaphor as far as I could. The character of Job remains a rich and personal one for all of us who want to know why innocent people suffer. He is confused; he is a fool. He looks for answers in the wrong places. But he keeps asking "why?" My Job is a man with a bright red nose and cream pies melting down his face. The fact that he would appear very differently to others is exactly what makes the Bible such a rich, creative source for theatrical ritual and musical composition.*

The following essay describes what inspired me to write Job. *It also delineates the various characters in the Book of Job and how I saw each as a clown type.*

(Biblical quotations are adapted from the King James Version; the "fairy tale" sections were written by Nessa Rapoport.)

The Story

There was a man in ancient land, his name was Job-Iov.
A perfect righteous honorable man, a man who feared his God.
He turned away from evil, he sought only the good.
A perfect righteous honorable man, a man who feared his God.
Now Job had ten children, three daughters and seven sons.
Seven thousand sheep in flock, camels three thousand strong.
Hundreds of oxen, hundreds of mules and servants manifold.
The richest man in all the land, the greatest man of all.
His sons would make a grand, grand feast, each in his own way.
And they used to send for their sisters and eat and drink all day.
When the days of feasting ceased, then Job rose early to sanctify
With sacrifices to offset any evil in their hearts or eyes.

I try to spend every New Year's Eve watching the beauty and antics of the Big Apple Circus. Unlike the larger and more flamboyant Ringling Brothers, the Big Apple has only one ring and an eccentric virtuoso array of ensemble performers. The animals are healthy and tolerant (the elephant pours champagne into a glass at midnight). The acrobats double as jugglers and stilt walkers. There's a family feeling. The ringmaster is an educated, strict father. His rebellious and hilarious children are, of course, the clowns.

Several years ago the Big Apple Circus introduced a master clown I'd never seen before. His name was Dimitri. Dimitri entered the ring during a blackout with only a sharp, angular spotlight shining on him. He pushed a cart full of boxes of instruments. He was dressed somewhat like a hobo, and his face had an orange, muddy pallor. He wasn't a sad sack. He seemed curiously serene. Every time he tried to move forward, the boxes on his cart fell to the dirt. He'd patiently rearrange them and they'd fall again. It took Dimitri a long time to get to the center of the ring, and once he arrived, his troubles had just begun. He unpacked the different instruments, but he had only parts of instruments— the mouthpiece of a trombone, the bell of a trumpet, the stem of a clarinet. He earnestly tried to put the parts together. He'd play and get a horrible honk or toot. He'd try the puzzle again and get a bray like a donkey or a wail like an elephant. Dimitri never lost patience. He ignored the laughter and the odds, which seemed stacked against him. When he finally got the trombone, trumpet, clarinet, tuba and flute assembled, he began to play an eerie, beautiful melody, moving rapidly from one instrument to another, never losing a beat. His melancholy and soulful tone reminded me of another clown I'd seen. At the end of Fellini's documentary *The Clowns* an elderly clown talks about his dead partner and how he summoned him by standing in the middle of the ring playing a trumpet duet they once used as a finale for their act. The film ends with a clown standing alone in front of empty bleachers in the mess left from a wild show. He plays a tune full of longing and humor. Another trumpet answers him from the darkness. He never questions the mystery. I copied down the notes just to see how the music came to have such an ethereal, calling melody. Of course there were no hints to the magic I'd heard in the bare musical notes. Years of experience and belief lived inside the old clown and his trumpet.

Watching Dimitri that New Year's Eve and hearing the Fellini music in my head, I found myself thinking of Job. This was a clown who sat in a spotlight, abandoned by all the others, left to deal with seemingly arbitrary tricks and hardships that were never resolved. He was patient, then frustrated, determined to solve his travails to the point of insanity, and his isolation was striking. I wondered if there wasn't some way to portray the story of Job as a clown show. Job and a clown had much in common. Disaster came for no apparent reason. The harder a clown tries to extricate himself from a catastrophe, the worse it gets. Clowns are often scorned by ringmasters or other clowns for getting into trouble. Anyone who tries to help the beleaguered clown usually manages to aggravate the situation. "Friends" get fed up and leave the exhausted clown to his own salvation. A clown has to exhibit enormous patience. If his pants keep falling down, he just has to keep pulling them up. A clown has to be tolerant. If he gets ten pies in the face, he has to endure ten more. If he asks why, he gets no answer. There didn't seem to be an answer as to why an elephant stepped on his foot and wouldn't move. If the pies stop or the other clowns stop hitting him with a big rubber bat, the timing of his redemption is as inexplicable as his persecution. A clown, it seems to me, is a character of great faith. He lives in a haphazard, cruel world and yet he makes no attempt to escape. He endures. It is his destiny to suffer. He has much in common with Job.

What kind of clown was Job? A low clown? Pies and rubber bats, raspberries and seltzer bottles? Or a more elevated Pierrot? Was he a Charlie Chaplin fighting the monster of an urban civilization? Or was he a Beckett character, a prisoner of a spotlight? Was he condemned to call out to characters who passed through his life, tempting him and scolding him but never stopping to offer salvation? Was he a Ringling Brothers clown, run over by a fire truck, squirted by seltzer, furious with his predicaments, unable, even in his rage, to get the abuse to stop? Or was he a passive target, a clown who set himself up to be the foil of "smarter clowns," accepting their taunts and oversized boxing gloves, too punch-drunk to fight for his dignity? Job was, at different times and for different reasons, all these clowns and more.

God and Satan

Now, there was a day when the angels of God stood before the Lord.
And Satan came within their midst.
God said to him: "From what chaos do you come?"
Satan answered and he said: "I am from the place of no rest.
To and fro upon the earth, walking up and down."
God said to him: "Have you set your sights on my servant named Job?
For there is none like him on earth, a perfect righteous good man.
A perfect man.
Fearing God, refuting ill, fearing God, refusing evil."
Then Satan answered God and said: "Why shouldn't Job fear you?
Look at the way you've buffered him with his house and all his goods,
Blessing the work of his hands, his worth increasing in all the land.
Stop, with your great hand smite all he has and you'll see:
Job will curse you to your face."

Job was the object of a practical joke. He was the patsy in a wager between God and Satan. Satan tells God, "I can get that goody-goody Job to lose faith in you." God says, "No, you can't." Satan says, "Oh, yes I can. Let me just take away his physical comforts and a few choice loved ones. He'll turn on you." God says, "Go, try." And the bet of the millennium begins. Job is a perfect setup for a foil. Innocent Job tends to his farm, family, and prayers and then suddenly, seemingly for no reason, messengers begin arriving. Each messenger brings worse news than the one before: "Your oxen are dead." "Your sheep are slain." "Your cattle stolen." "Your servants murdered." "Your house burned down." "Your children all crushed to death." The messengers arrive in rapid succession, and each one is the only one left to tell his macabre, ridiculously gory story. Job watches this Indianapolis 500 of cruelty and keeps waiting for the racers to stop running over him. And you want to say, "So what's the punch line?" But there is none. It's a merciless shaggy-dog story.

Job's wife becomes a shrew clown. She could wear a red wig and wield an oversized bowling pin. "This is ridiculous," she seems to say. "Curse God and die." Bam! She hits him over the head with the bowling pin. But Job, though off balance and disoriented, is a patient clown. Tattered, blown apart, and humiliated, he sticks to his little place in the ring. He savors the quiet after the mad production number. He grieves to the audience, tearing off his tie and coattails, trying to get his high hat back on his head. He does what he can with his broken props. "Naked I came from my mother's womb," he says. "And naked I'll return. God gave. God has taken. May the Lord's name be a blessing."

The Boils

Again the day came when the angels of God stood before the Lord. And Satan, too, came in their midst, he too before his God. God said to him: "Where are you coming from?" And Satan answered him to say: "To and fro, to and fro. Up and down, up and down."

God said to Satan: "Have you set your heart on my servant named Job? None like him in all the land, a perfect righteous honorable man. Fearing God, resisting evil, holding fast to his purity. Despite your setting me against him within and without reason."

Satan replied to God and said: "His faith is just skin deep. A man will give all he has to breathe, just to save his life. Put forth your hand, smite bone, tear flesh and he will curse you to your face."

Satan and God witness Job's resiliency and Satan ups the ante in this heavenly bet. He explains to God that Job will stay faithful until his own physical well-being is threatened. Now the method of clown technique must change. We have used simple methods until now, employing mostly bad dancing, tasteless melodrama, and goofy "corpses" falling over Job like sacks of flour. Now, however, the slapstick has to get more disgusting. We have to combine horror movies and the Three Stooges. We must combine the relentless physical abuse of Abbott and Costello with the scatological excesses of Jonathan Swift. We stop the narrative here and ask, "What horrendous, disgusting thing can Satan do to Job's body?" Children have no qualms about participating in the fantasies of really uncensored torture. We've seen it all in wrestling matches, in wars, in famine, in natural and man-made catastrophes and ancient and modern plagues. So we twist Job's nose, hack at his limbs, pull out his hair, elbow his private parts, operate on his belly button with a chain saw, pound a stake into his heart, turn his head 360 degrees, push a drumstick in one ear and out the other, and he screeches and hops and gags and does a pratfall. In the Bible Job ends up with a nasty case of boils all over his skin. Our boils are balloon boils filled with water, tied all over him and ripe for popping. But despite the abuse and his extreme physical discomfort, Job simply must endure. He has to keep the show going for reasons he can't understand. Despite all that's happened, Job's horrible nightmare has barely begun. He's only at the end of his first act. For him there's no sense of absolute time. No beginning. No end. A clown lives to survive the present. Each second is as full as a whole life. Each moment is so important, it seems as if it will never pass. A clown never knows when his ordeal will be over. By being a clown he's relinquished the control of his life to the unknown forces. The attacks on him come from every direction, but the clown can't uncover a central force that gives the orders. He can complain his heart out, but each stranger to whom he brings his complaint doesn't understand, or is repelled by his hideous physical state. The line between nightmare and comedy can become very thin. Job the clown can ask *why* his life is in shambles, but his chances of getting an answer from a source he trusts are probably nonexistent. He doesn't know what he did that made the bucket fall on his head. He doesn't know why the bucket is there or if it's ever coming off. Some clowns don't even know they have buckets on their heads and therefore can't figure out why they keep walking into walls. Some clowns don't know how scary their bizarre infirmities are and why they bring screams from other clowns who see them. If they chance upon a mirror, they'll cry out in terror and run from their own reflection. They've become so bulbous or withered—the gag is they don't recognize themselves.

The Friends

Call now; is there any one who will answer you? To which of the holy ones will you turn? Surely vexation kills the fool, and jealousy slays the simple. I have seen the fool taking root, but suddenly I cursed his dwelling. His sons are far from safety, they are crushed in the gate, and there is no one to deliver them. His harvest the hungry eat, and he takes it even out of thorns; and the thirsty pant after his wealth. For affliction does not come from the dust, nor does trouble sprout from the ground; but man is born to trouble as the sparks fly upward.

Job isn't a one-man clown show. There are other characters written into the text who have their entrances and exits with the specific purpose of making a really bad situation worse. These characters are like early sitcom clowns—*I Love Lucy*, Jackie Gleason, Burns and Allen clowns of the Bible. They have lots of passion, a million ideas, and they get hot under the collar if Job doesn't see their point of view. These "friends" want to help Job get past his sorrow, get rid of his ugly boils, reconcile his relationship with his wife and regain his riches. They're so determined to help Job that they have no desire to listen to what he has to say. His opinions can't be worth much anyway—if he got himself in such a predicament. These friends fall under the category of bulldozer clowns—they're bound and determined to get Job off the window ledge even if it means pushing him off. They're going to pull his head out of the potted plant even if it means stretching him like a rubber band. They're going to get Job to stop crying even if it means scaring him to death and replacing the tears with hiccups. They're the kinds of friends whose sympathy is rooted in disapproval, mild distaste, and in some cases downright fury. Job needs them like a hole in the head, but since he's been assigned the role of the dupe, he must willingly or even unwillingly take the advice of each of them and be put through the ordeal of each "cure."

Eliphaz

Behold, happy is the man whom God reproves; therefore despise not the chastening of the Almighty. For he wounds, but he binds up; he smites, but his hands heal. He will deliver you from six troubles; in seven there shall no evil touch you. In famine he will redeem you from death, and in war from the power of the sword. You shall be hid from the scourge of the tongue.

Eliphaz is the first friend. He is the car mechanic, physician, fix-it clown. His beliefs seem to be rooted in the notion that Job has something fundamentally wrong with him, or he wouldn't have lost everything and be caught in this tragic drama. To Eliphaz Job is like a defective car or a broken-down human machine. Look inside, check the oil, bounce the springs, pull out the engine, electrocute him by charging his battery, poison him by giving him gasoline, slam his hood, kick his tires, staple a bill to his chest, and send him on his way. Eliphaz is a friend who believes strongly in cause and effect. If he gives Job a tune-up, if Job's mechanism runs according to the fundamental laws of mechanics, he won't break down. Job might try to tell Eliphaz that there's nothing fundamentally wrong with him—he did nothing *wrong*. But no doubt Eliphaz has his rubber flashlight stuck so far down Job's throat, he can't hear. When he pulls the sausage and the telephone from Job's innards, he is convinced Job's parts are tainted. Eliphaz would like to wrench the very heart from Job, but despite Eliphaz's huge chain saw and blowtorch, Job's exhausted heart stubbornly stays in place. The frustrated mechanic doesn't regard Job as a very cooperative or high-class specimen.

This is a case where the operation becomes much more important than the patient. As a "friend" Eliphaz is a well-meaning clown and doesn't realize he's nearly killing Job in the search to find out what's wrong with him. Eliphaz tries to have compassion—or at least pity—but these are not emotions that last long in clowns like Eliphaz. If Job can't cough up enough proof of his sin, Eliphaz isn't going to listen to Job's cries of pain. Better to solder his teeth together. This loyal friend decides that if Job continues to insist there's nothing wrong with him, it's time to dump him in the human junkyard.

Bildad

How long will you say these things, and the words of your mouth be a great wind? Does God pervert justice? Or does the Almighty pervert the right your children have sinned against him, he has delivered them into the power of their transgression. If you will seek God and make supplication to the Almighty, if you are pure and upright, surely then he will rouse himself for you and reward you with a rightful habitation. And though your beginning was small, your latter days will be very great.

The second "friend" who appears is Bildad. Bildad is not worried about the past or Job's fundamental make-up. Bildad is a discipline freak. He knows how Job should behave. He has the formula to turn a terrible, sinful life into a four-star redemption. Job tries to tell Bildad that he hasn't lived a terrible life and there's no *reason* to partake in bizarre purification rituals and punishing exercise to become a more zealous, patriotic person. Bildad, however, seems to be dedicated to the notion of punishment before the crime. He's a cross between an army commander and an aerobics instructor gone mad. He's the fascist clown. He wants to teach Job how to be a man, how to take his punches and how to be aggressively holy. He has Job run laps, do push-ups, march with his chest out, pull in his abdomen until it juts out his back. Bildad extinguishes a burning cigarette in Job's bare palm and warns him not to cry. He teaches him to do lethal rifle maneuvers while making vicious guard dogs out of balloons. Bildad is busy being paranoid watching Job's every position and move. He's totally immersed in rules, regulations, CV, body building, manliness, preparedness, and violence. He is God's little drill sergeant. He thinks he should train the wimpiness out of Job in one session. Once Bildad sees that Job is nearly dead from overexertion, he's overjoyed and encouraged. But after further testing Bildad feels a sense of hopelessness about Job's testosterone. The exhausted clown can only make a little duck out of his balloon, not a ferocious rifle.

Whereas Bildad thrusts, Job can only quack. Bildad knows that those who are less physically pure and perfect are not worthy of God's attention. Job's intellectual whininess forces Bildad to stomp on Job's head for his own good.

Zophar

Can you find out the deep things of God? Can you find out the limit of the Almighty? It is higher than heaven—what can you do? Deeper than She-ol—what can you know? Its measure is longer than the earth, and broader than the sea. If he passes through, and imprisons, and calls to judgment, who can hinder him? For he knows worthless men; when he sees iniquity, will he not consider it?

The third visiting ally is Zophar. He's calm about Job's predicament. He seems less emotionally involved. He doesn't care about Job's mechanical diseases or his inability to follow specific rules. Zophar surmises that Job is genetically inferior. Most human beings by nature come with defective cells, inferior nerves, and faulty electronic fields. Zophar is the guru-scientist clown. He advises that Job abandon any notion of his own importance and see himself as a recipe of mixed-up molecules. His pain is not pain—it is a gross misunderstanding of science. Job can't feel better because it is useless to try to be a weak human. Feelings are so low on the scale of things. Even worms know that messy emotions have nothing to do with God. God likes props, advanced word processors, and Nintendo games. Man is a glorious calculation. And Job is nothing more than a severely miscalculated mathematical equation. Zophar—as scientist—will use computers and electronic inventions to rearrange Job's atoms and circuitry. He decides to join him genetically with a brainless surfer from northern California and find the right mix of DNA and spam for both of them. The Zophar clown is obsessed with the big picture. He has no time for the little puzzle parts of human beings. What he cares about are the data of his experimentation. Whatever is sacrificed toward the final mathematical proof is a gift to science. Zophar's scientific device short-circuits, and he ends up with the surfer's brain while the surfer goes off to Big Sur to contemplate genetic engineering. The computers blow up. Body parts fly all over. Job is left as unchanged and as frazzled as an overcooked French fry. His clothes are burned. He's in shock. His "friends" are exhausting whatever was left of his endurance. He has only his same tears and prayers. He's even more desperate and alone.

Elihu

I am young in years, and you are aged; therefore I was timid and afraid to declare my opinion to you. I said, "Let days speak, and many years teach wisdom." But it is the spirit in a man, the breath of the Almighty, that makes him understand. It is not the old that are wise, nor the aged that understand what is right. Therefore I say, "Listen to me; let me also declare my opinion." Behold, I waited for your words, I listened for your wise sayings, while you searched out what to say. I gave you my attention, and, behold, there was none that confuted Job, or that answered his words, among you. Beware lest you say, "We have found wisdom; God may vanquish him, not man." He has not directed his words against me, and I will not answer him with your speeches.

Elihu makes no pretense about being Job's friend. He lets us know that he disdains the filthy, old, beaten-up has-been of a clown. Elihu is young and handsome, a lady-killer who knows magic tricks. He's the showoff clown. If there is anyone who would provoke Job to feel envy—

it would be Elihu. Elihu's the type of guy who claims to have seen God. Elihu can catch bubbles on the end of his tongue and turn them into crystal balls, while Job gets a mouthful of soap. Elihu can transform his cape into a cane and dance a dazzling tap dance. Job's rags remain rags and his oversized shoes cause him to fall. Elihu is a fire-eater. He breathes fire like a dragon. Job breathes dust and has an asthma attack. Elihu is young. Job is old. Elihu is cocky. Job can't keep up with his hip-hop dance steps. Elihu claims to be loved by God and understands perfectly why God does what he does. It is the young who take over God's love because the has-beens no longer know how to listen. Worst of all, Elihu doesn't care one way or another about Job. Elihu's the future. He's got the present in his fingertips (colored confetti, sparks, streamers) and he is the future. If Job can't pull himself together, well, that's too bad, Elihu's got Job's act covered with God. Elihu is the performer's worst nightmare. Life goes on without us. Someone steps in who is as good as we were—maybe better. There's no evidence that we'll be remembered or missed. The scariest part of watching Elihu perform his Romeo-clown magic is that, by comparison, Job's suffering seems very dull. "It's been done," Elihu seems to say. "You haven't had a hit in years. You give others nothing with your doubts and lamentations. It's time for some entertainment. I've got the funding from God and I know what show he wants to see. My sold-out show is being extended. Your closing notice is long overdue."

Job's Lamentations

Let the day perish wherein I was born, and the night which said, "A man-child is conceived." Let that day be darkness! May God above not seek it, nor light shine upon it. Let gloom and deep darkness claim it. Let clouds dwell upon it; let the blackness of the day terrify it. That night—let thick darkness seize it! Let it rejoice among the days of the year, let it not come into the number of the months.

In between each visit of Eliphaz, Bildad, Zophar and Elihu, the Job clown tries to figure out how he ended up in the middle of this circus ducking pies and being hitched up to the contraptions of his "friends."

He doesn't just weep and moan. Like any good clown, he attempts to make the best of his situation. He tries, like Red Skelton, to chase the spotlight that keeps evading him. He begs for a way to end his misery. He offers to make bargains and deals and, looking like a madman, babbles to the nothingness around him. He loses his temper, regains control, and loses his temper again. Like the mythological clowns of ancient Africa and Native American tricksters, Job's body and mind fight within him. He is a creature forced into a war with himself—his right hand fighting his left, his fingers tearing at his hair as if he were a foreign enemy.

In the Bible, Job's lamentations are exquisite, dark poems of suffering. They might not seem appropriate as texts for the songs of a clown. But clowns are not the stereotypical buffoons that many audiences imagine. There's a reason why many children are as afraid of them as love them. The white-faced, red-nosed clown is as potent a nightmare image as an entertaining bozo. He's an extreme. He's on the edge of what's real. No one knows what he really will do. Or what will be done to him. You push a funny routine one step beyond the ridiculous and you may end up with real cruelty. You take a pratfall and keep the clown's body prone for one minute too long and he could be dead. You shoot him out of a cannon and he could go too high and float forever in weightless darkness. A child's mind knows this. A child also knows that the clown's mask covers a human face. The mystery of the relationship between the clown's painted mask and the flesh underneath can be as haunting as the masks of a Greek drama or an African masquerade. Into what world are we going? What is this creature who leads us? What is the relation between my dreams and this odd, distorted, beautiful face?

Therefore, the lamentations of Job introduce another kind of clown to the stage. He's the same man, but he inhabits a markedly different world of clowns. These are the victims of ancient tricksters. They've been seduced, duped, and tormented as innocents in mythology for centuries. They show up in Indian, Native American, Balinese and African ritual. This behavior is not unlike characters related through parables as told by the Baal Shem Tov or the creators of classic fairy tales. They have the resigned wisdom of Lear's fool. Their counterparts suffered and endured, convinced and transcended in war zones and camps everywhere, including Eastern Europe, Germany, Cambodia, Central America, Somalia, and Ethiopia. Wherever men and women have been victimized by unspeakable evil, there are characters who faced their undoing as hero-clowns. With concrete weapons or abstract literary meditations, these clowns fight against impossible odds. They try to advance the cause of goodness simply by fighting. They refuse to let evil prevail, and sometimes eloquent suffering is their only defense. It's the impossible, overwhelming odds that make them clowns. It's the seeming arbitrariness of the cruelties they encounter that transform them into symbols of David-like "smallness" or "nothingness" as compared with the omnipresent forces of fate or the gods they face. Universal images bring these clowns to mind: the tiny, weakened worker bent under a crushing load; the last man on the breadline who waits and waits only to arrive at the front to find the bread all gone; the slave who lifts rocks from one side of the road to another, only to turn around and lift them back over the road again; the farmer who plants the single fruit and watches it plucked by his greedy overseer; the beaten man who attacks a lurking shadow and finds it is his own reflection; the starving child searching through garbage; the slave singing under the whip of the overseer; the woman who sings the lullaby to the broken child, half knowing the child can't hear her, her face frozen in an immortal clown mask of grief. This is a very different style of mime. Job the clown becomes witness and participant in these and other photographs of disaster, which come to life and haunt him.

An unexpected illness or injury can come off like a bad joke. A mourner can feel like the victim of a conspiracy of invisible forces. The "conspiracy" feels like a bet between Satan and God. Job had no clue he'd become the central player in an unfathomable show about pain and loss. He was the leading man and he hadn't known he'd been cast. He's an unwilling guest at a party in which all the other guests are mad. Or he is the only madman in a village where it doesn't seem moral to remain sane. But although he contemplates suicide again and again, he never acts on his threats. It isn't hope that keeps him going. He keeps going because that seems to be his assignment or fate. Clowns are innately stubborn. They may not consciously challenge their oppressors. Few clowns openly declare war on the forces that make shambles out of their simple lives. Nonetheless they hang on. They endure insult upon insult, beating upon beating, loss upon loss. Their energy for accepting humiliation is indefatigable, and therefore they turn humiliation into something noble. The well of their tears is deep. When you watch a great clown, you feel as if he's lived out his battle with the rubber bat, the bucket, and the pie forever. You sense that it will go on forever. This is the clown's service. He's a shaman for the audience, taking on their worst fears, accepting derision for their mistakes. He grieves the audience's grief and takes in the pain an audience has suffered. When the night is over, the audience, spent from laughter, experiences relief from tension and anger. No one knows what a clown feels. You'd never get a straight answer from a real clown.

Of course clowns do scream for relief. By the time thirty pies have been thrown in Job's face, he would demand an explanation. "Why me? Why not Eliphaz, Bildad, or the clown on the unicycle or the one on the donkey?" The silence that meets Job's entreaties makes his temper seem all the more ridiculous. A lonely clown shaking his fist in an empty tent yelling at the empty sky is a perfect image of madness. But Job can't lose his mind completely, because then he wouldn't feel the excruciating pain he's meant to feel. If he went insane, he'd enter a new reality, and it seems he's doomed to suffer without illusion. His desolation and confusion never overwhelm him to the point where he loses his ability to describe clearly what's going on. He can't withdraw— the spotlight's on him. He sinks as low as any human being can go, but he must rally. The show must go on and on and on.

The Voice of God

Where were you when I laid the foundation of the earth? Tell me, if you have understanding. Who determined its measurements—surely you know! Or who stretched the line upon it? Have you commanded the morning since your day began, and caused the dawn to know its place, that it might take hold of the skirts of the earth, and the wicked be shaken out of it? Have you entered into the springs of the sea, or walked in the recesses of the deep? Have the gates of death been revealed to you, or have you seen the gates of deep darkness? Have you comprehended the expanse of the earth? Declare if you know all this. Where is the way to the dwelling of light, and where is the place of darkness?

Can you lift up your voice to the clouds, that a flood of waters may cover you? Can you send forth lightnings, that they may go and say to you, "Here we are?" Who has put wisdom in the clouds, or given understanding to the mists?

Finally Job receives the biggest pie in the face of all. Without introduction, warning, trumpets, angels or reason, God pops out of nowhere and speaks to him. The lights change, and the whole set is overtaken by a booming voice. Job isn't even given the benefit of smoke, flashpots, or a burning bush. God just resonates like a huge rock 'n' roll speaker. Furthermore God isn't giving any clear-cut answers for the bizarre events that have distinguished Job's existence. God in effect shouts at Job through a megaphone saying, "You can't know the universe, clown, so don't try to understand where you fit into it." God is like the ringmaster, rushing onstage, ready to bring on the horses and elephants, and he finds, to his surprise and dismay, that there's still one clown left mopping the floor. The ringmaster is impatient and unsympathetic. He has a whole circus to get going. The curtains are opening, the orchestra starts to play, and the ringmaster wants to restore the stage to its original, colorful, active chaos. The clown's lonely spotlight is snapped off, and he's expected to resume his place among his large family of entertainers.

Job is supposed to accept this change in reality without question. He is after all only a clown. He goes where he's directed. Maybe it takes a couple of kicks in the pants by the ringmaster, but he has a whole night ahead of him. He must juggle, walk on stilts, dance to the accordion exactly as he did before. Maybe he is rewarded by getting to watch his friends, Eliphaz and the others, fall in the mud instead of him. Maybe the ringmaster gives him balloons, a short bow, and some whistles from the audience. But Job's personal travail is over. The transformation occurs as inexplicably as it began. Job has no choice but

70

to accept these startling changes. He can't ask about the timing of his redemption or even if the idea of bad and good have anything to do with it. He simply has to move with the flow of the action. He will take his part in the lovely parade of acrobats and animals as fully as he did when he railed against his broken suspenders or blown-up tricycle. His painted mouth will turn upward, with its sad smile glowing toward the girl on the trapeze. And the smile will be as real as his grimace when he caught the dead dummy someone shot at him from a cannon. The smile doesn't seem to remember the frown. Job no longer seems to have any passion to fight God's ways. Satan isn't even mentioned. Maybe he was paid by the hour. The wisest choice for Job is not a choice at all. He's relinquished his desire for control. The universe is far more cruel and complex than the logic of a tiny man with a painted face. He travels through a dangerous and arbitrary expanse of time never knowing what will happen to him or when. He keeps facing the unknown. This is what makes him a hero. And this is why many heroes are clowns and why Job lives inside any person who has innocently suffered.

But Job lived for many years—a hundred and another forty—and saw his sons and his son's sons, four generations procreating. The daughters, each in their own way, were stunned by that which once befell him. And no one knew if they would marry, or ever bear children. Despite the fact that Job did die at a great and venerable age, his daughters knew what the songs forgot: that all you have can be whirled away. Naked we stand before our God, naked born and then return. Made of earth, days like grass, and all we own returns with us. The portion of the righteous thus: Comfort that we are but dust.

Being the Director (2006)

It's difficult to be a director and *not* be a director at the same time. On the one hand, you want to set up a structure that keeps the work organized and safe. But the goal, in this instance, is also to impart the specific mechanics of the theater process to your students, and let them pull apart and remake technique and tradition. You want to give a sense of how arduous it is to put together a show, and at the same time make the students hungry to rewrite the rules. You want to teach specific skills while simultaneously encouraging freedom of the imagination. You must impose strict discipline while bringing forth uninhibited energy.

You, as the director, are the one who teaches the exercises, leads the discussions, and sets forth the ideas of form, theme, and content. But I've discovered from years of leading adolescent groups that you have to become a teacher who denies being a teacher and a leader who never dictates or pontificates. You have to be able to change course in a second and, like a jazz improviser, alter the direction of the work according to the student's energy and moods. In this work there are no ultimatums. Students either choose on their own to take the risk or not (and some won't choose right away, so you have to be patient).

Even if you are a teacher in a school, teaching in a classroom, it's up to you to make your students' theater experiences different from day-to-day classes. All directors of young people have to be highly aware and energized themselves, for the role of a director is to make the actors want to participate and dig deep inside for the best of themselves. A director doesn't "make" students perform. She creates a whole atmosphere that is conducive to humor, exploration, and taking risks. She is a benign gang leader. In fact, she has to be the most intense performer of all—and then be willing to disappear.

I go on about this because a large percentage of what makes good directing is letting go of expectations. If you come into a project already knowing what a show is, who's cast in what role, what the blocking is, and what the interpretation will be, then very few of the exercises I present will be helpful to you. That style of directing involves a very different kind of method and ego. The theater I am writing about requires that you believe your students have inside them the potential to make theater of their own. You have to truly want to *listen* to them. No matter how sullen or nervous or withdrawn they are at the start, you have to know that something powerful and interesting will come out. As a director, your investment is in creating great theater, and therefore you must stay absolutely dedicated to the health and vision of your students.

So don't try to dress like a homeboy, but perhaps dress down a little for the occasion. Create an atmosphere that is comfortable and personal so your students will feel more at ease than they do in the schoolroom every day. And announce the rules right from the start so that the boundaries are clear and the work doesn't become about enforcing them. These are the rules I set up for my actors before every workshop or rehearsal period:

1. I designate a spot in the room that is "holy." That's where we'll do exercises and improvs. I make a circle within that space and keep that circle sacred. Everywhere else should have the feel of freedom, where you can have pillows, popcorn, or posters, but that particular space and circle are not to be messed with.

2. No attitude. My message to actors is: You mouth off to me or someone else in the group or disrespect the work and you're out.

3. I care very much about how your day-to-day lives affect you, but I won't allow moods and acting out during the workshop hours. Before and after hours, you can have all my attention and I'll do everything I can to listen to you and help you. But your job is not to bring your troubles into the circle or even the rehearsal room.

4. You will not criticize or make fun of one another's work. First of all, it's rude, and second, you don't know enough.

5. You have to trust I won't make a fool of you or myself.

6. No violence, drugs, or alcohol.

7. No romantic or sexual behavior in the room.

I think anyone who aspires to be a director or teacher must

find objectivity within himself or herself that transcends habitual categorizations of young people. You can't have a personal agenda if you want to serve the show's best interests. Instead, you have to find a way to neutralize your likes and dislikes, and in that way strive to be as open and devoid of censorship as you hope your students will be. If you can achieve this level of objectivity, you'll be constantly surprised that individuals who make up your ensemble and the ensemble as a whole will grow stronger. This kind of energy creates shows and performances that work for audiences in two ways: they feel the depth of the stories and character and also unconsciously absorb the unified and committed spirit of the cast.

Think of times when you've been in a group or classroom led by an individual who was overbearing or who allowed chaos. Now think of who inspired you, and made you want the hours never to end.

Finally, I see no advantage to forcing a young actor to reach deep down into his gut, to share the unrecognized agonizing terrors and abuses of his life. I know this might seem odd, considering I often work in areas of child abuse, violence, and loss. Even so, I think unlimited personal confessions are extremely dangerous in the younger years. As theater artists and teachers, none of us are qualified to deal with the consequences of provoking a troubled child or teenager—or any child or teenager, for that matter—as he plunges into a nightmarish reliving of terror or pain. It's especially tempting to turn issue-oriented theater work into bad therapy, but bad therapy makes bad theater. I believe that if you work for the good of the artist—for the quality of the show—you are actually getting deeper truths from each individual. In my rehearsals I always say, "Tell me a story about a time when something happened, it doesn't matter if it's true, just make it a good story." Or "Let me see a character..." and then I advise them to create the character through the body and the voice — even if the character is the student herself.

In those rare moments when you can't help scaring or upsetting the actors, stay in control of the time you take. For instance, if I'm staging a disturbing scene with violence or death, I do it once and then I don't repeat the scene until some time later. Once the kids know it's part of a whole, that's fine, but the initial staging of a dark moment, if it's good, may feel too real. When we were making my show called *The Violence Project*, we spent several hours making horrific images that required buckets of fake blood, but we also did slapstick and improvs about the fact that it was indeed fake. I balanced horrible images with horrible humor. If we are telling upsetting stories, I allow for five or six stories and then move on to something more physical. And after we experience what might be a heartbreaking and scary day, at the end of rehearsal I always put on loud music so everyone can dance.

After I establish the rules, I then have to get the young actors used to "being directed," which is very different from being taught. They have to hear me with not just their ears but also their bodies. They have to understand quickly and expect rapid changes.

II. Some Actors

Amani, *Runaways* (1979)

I saw a very tall sullen teenager dressed in an all black karate suit. He had his hair in messy cornrows. His face was exceptionally beautiful with large eyes and the high proud cheekbones I'd seen in the Fulani tribe in the desert. I'd never seen anyone skateboard like him. Where most other boys crashed up railings and did noisy flips, this boy moved with unexpected grace. He had long arms and legs like a dancer and rolled around on his skateboard making breathtaking spins and then high leaps as in ballet. There was a crowd surrounding him and he was quite aware of it. He dared to do riskier moves for applause.

I asked him to sit down with me and he sprawled out on a green bench. He gave me a broad teenager's grin, but his eyes were empty.

"You're amazing at that," I said.

He shrugged.

"Would you like to be in a show?" I asked him.

He bolted up. "Yeah," he said. "Does it pay?"

"It does," I told him. I gave him the time and the address of the loft and my phone number.

"What's your name?" I asked him.

He shrugged again. "Bernie Allison," he said.

"Where do you live?" I asked him.

"I used to have a place with my aunt, but I'm moving," he said. "I'm not sure yet."

I realized I was losing him. Never try to pin down a homeless kid.

"I'm vegan," he said.

"I don't know what that is."

He went into a long monologue about nutrition and amino acids, vitamins, cells, but it was running on and on and he was becoming incoherent.

"Show me what you do again," I said.

He did some of his dance moves for me.

"I'm the best in the city, but I'd never enter a contest," he said.

We parted ways.

Six months later he was dressed in a completely white karate suit and had changed his name to Amani Asani. His cornrows had become plaits with different colored rubber bands. He played with the younger boys and I noticed once that there were large perpendicular scars on his back where he'd been beaten and burned. He never talked about himself and was distracted and uninterested when others talked about problems with family. I assigned him to choreograph a whole solo for himself for *Runaways*. He'd invented this impossible move where he leaned forward balancing on the front of the board and seemed to be weeping with his sneakered feet on the wood. I'd never seen another skateboarder approach that kind of balance. I never knew where he slept or what he ate for dinner. But he hugged me now and then and smelled of vegetables. He was one of the stars of *Runaways*. He acquired many new outfits and many new friends, but his eyes were never anything but empty.

Geena and Nameless Punks, *Swing* (1987, BAM)

In the mid-eighties, there was a kind of plague going around where punk kids were particularly picking on elderly people. I wanted to create a show that would bring the very old and teenagers together and see if there was more going on than just base cruelty. I put together a fifteen-piece big band orchestra of players under sixteen and a group of ballroom dancers over seventy. The musicians were extraordinary. One nine-year-old saxophone player was removed from after school rehearsals because he had to play late sets every night. That put my back up.

Also I cast the most tame punks I could find who might not bust up the relative peace between the big band and elderly dancers. I didn't know where I was going exactly, but the Brooklyn Academy of Music at that time was very supportive of abstract imagery. One young couple I found was in a squatters' apartment on the Lower East Side. Dressed in uniform goth, she led him around as he crawled on his hands and his knees. He wore a spike collar around his neck attached to a chain that she pulled. I made them promise to do no violence to each other or anyone else or they wouldn't get paid and would be fired. Money works wonders on fourteen-year-olds. Besides the musical prodigies from Westchester, there was also a black kid of about twelve who lived in the notorious welfare hotel across from BAM. (There were murders there, and one day someone threw an uzi out a window). *New York Magazine* did a feature on the boy in the hotel, and the kid got a scholarship. He sang magnificently. Hopefully he got out of there for good although he was blatantly over the top gay and was going to meet up with other problems.

One of the punks I hired was a sexy looking fifteen-year-old girl, Geena. She had long dark hair and the green eyes of a cat. She was always on time and tried to be a good actress. But she seemed vaguely bored all the time, or distracted. Finally her "best friend" in the project approached me and said, "You really got to talk to her. She's gonna get in real trouble." So I took her into a corner and said, "Such and such is really worried about you." She gave me her cat smile and rolled her eyes. "It's no big deal," she said. "I'm doing good in school, I just don't get no sleep."

"Why?" I asked her.

She stared at me a long time.

"I go out," she said. "I stay out too late."

I felt completely inept.

"You need your sleep," I said.

She laughed and put her hand with its purple nail polish on my wrist.

"I been going out since I was ten," she said.

"Can't you stop? You're smart. You've got a future."

"Pays more than this," she said.

She came back to rehearsal the next day and everyday after that, despite the circles under her eyes.

Once or twice she winked at me.

"I'm having a real good time," she said.

Luis, *Loss and Gain* (2003)

I was doing a show called *Loss and Gain* in response to the shock of the World Trade Center. I auditioned a large variety of teenagers from thirteen to twenty-one. I cast kids who'd lost parents in the disaster and a boy who'd lost his older brother in a drive-by shooting. I cast kids whose parents had divorced or just kids who wanted to act and sing and demonstrated kindness, empathy and talent. Anyway the show was to be about all kinds of loss and gain, not only extreme tragedy. To my surprise, a football player from Canarsie High School auditioned. He was a big guy, half Latino, shy and barely said a word. I didn't think he knew why he was there anymore than I did, but I cast him anyway. I'd never worked with a junior varsity athlete before.

It turned out to be a disaster. He couldn't hold a tune. He couldn't dance. He had nothing in common with the other kids and I knew he was going to quit. "Listen Luis," I said to him. "Make up a dance that's all football moves. Whatever you do. Run, pass, tackle, push-ups, whatever."

The next day he came in with a series of moves that was really graceful and full of different shapes and forms. He thought it was stupid and awful, but I made him teach it to the whole cast and the outcome looked like a fully choreographed dance. The girls laughed at the idea of throwing imaginary passes or crashing into the floor, but actually had a great time. Luis's spirits picked up. He was getting teased by his team for doing drama, but when he showed off some of the hip-hop he was learning, his friends let up on him. He also wrote a monologue about what it felt like to catch a difficult pass and make a goal. "Gain," he said. "That was gain."

He stayed in the group until he graduated high school and went on to community college. He took drama courses there, but quit. They wanted him to learn Shakespeare and no matter how much I begged him he said it made him feel like a faggot.

The Remarkable Girl, *The Greek Trilogy* (1972)

She was six or seven when she quietly followed her burly cabdriver father into the tiny basement of La Mama. She had round light blue eyes, a perfect nose and a slightly pouty mouth. She was too scared to smile. But her audition went perfectly. Andrei Serban and I were creating a version of *Medea* that would be in Sophocles' Latin and Euripides' Ancient Greek. We wanted the sounds to convey the range of wildly dangerous emotions, not addled English translations. We were looking for a little girl who could perform as one of the innocent children Medea murders to get revenge on her unfaithful husband Jason. It's hard to explain to a little girl that she is going to be killed. But she said in a husky voice, "My father already explained it to me."

It turned out that her mother was in Florida and the father had brought them both to New York to see if the little girl could get commercial jobs. He subsidized their adventure by driving a cab and teaching theater. She was serious and quick. I taught her the Greek— "*Kamoi Kat Kamoon*"—and she picked up the long vowels and sharp consonants instantly. The other part of the audition was to walk straight across a carpet with perfect posture and no bumps or stops. Her stillness was eerie. It was as if she'd been studying Noh drama for years. Andrei, the twenty-six-year-old prodigious director, was fascinated by her. But I was worried that between school and the show, she'd get sick. She had brown circles under her eyes. For the next three years she was executed by Medea every night all around the world. Her poise and sweetness never left her. Sometimes when her father wasn't around and the traveling became too much for her, she wept and wept and no one could comfort her. Then she'd pull herself together as if acting was what she had decided to do and she wasn't about to disappoint her colleagues, father, or herself. The entire company of *Medea* (there were eight to ten, plus Andrei and myself) brought her up. She was our child and by the time she was ten she'd seen Europe, Eastern Europe and the Mideast. Her maturity grew and she was a serious girl who worked very hard with her father and her tutor on her studies.

Once *Medea* ended, she took other parts and approached them with the same dedication and natural gifts. She was a born actress. I included her automatically in the cast of *Runaways* and once again, she concentrated only on her studies and her role as a child prostitute. She was thirteen. She didn't hang out with the other kids and had few special friends. If she was lonely she never showed it. I remember once she was studying owls and she showed me her report and accompanying illustrations. It was one of the few times I saw her smile. Whenever I see an owl I think of her. Whenever I see her now I know she was a born actress with talents that contained truthfulness and an almost religious dedication. She, Diane Lane, is a famous movie star now and deserves to be. We will always love each other. We grew up together. She, I think, more than me.

Nameless JT, *The Violence Project* (2002)

I found him through a great organization called The Door which deals with all kinds of kids in every area of their lives from health, to drug abuse, to safe sex, to counseling, arts and crafts, creation, writing, drama. They protect kids and help find them homes. In the seventies and eighties, I thought they were the most exemplary loving example of a second home for any kind of kid, troubled or just restless. I wished I could go there.

The Door let me do a big audition where I must've talked to thirty kids in one small room. We did improvisations, singing, rhythms and I encouraged them to talk about what they felt about the times they lived in. Not personal confession. I never force or coerce personal confession.

I was doing a show based on violence because it had been a particularly grisly year of gang fights and drive-by shootings as well as domestic abuse and family killings. I was auditioning at community houses and schools all over the place and, for reasons I'll never figure out, an extremely menacing Latino boy excelled at the audition. I cast him and he actually came to rehearsal.

When the cast did physical warm-ups and used sounds the kid stood at the side with his arms folded, leaning against the wall. He wouldn't make eye contact. And yet he came every day took up the same stance and watched as we advanced in hip-hop moves, stretches, singing, rap. And the kids were beginning to write about violence they'd seen or experienced. I still didn't know the kid's name and he wouldn't make eye contact with me. "Alright," I thought. "I won't make eye contact with you." From that moment on I stopped looking at him.

That went on for a few days and then one afternoon I turned around and our eyes locked. He smiled. So did I. It was a sort of nasty "Gotcha" moment on both our sides. The next day I entered his space by the wall and asked him his name.

"J.T.," he said.

"Why are you here if you don't do anything?" I asked.

"I take my time," J.T. said. He was a really scary kid with slicked back hair, the beginning of a mustache, a scar on his cheek and deep-set brown eyes that both hated and were amused by everything he saw.

I noticed, however, that when he thought no one was watching, he fidgeted and fixed his hair and pulled at his T-shirt like a twelve-year-old. At those moments he just seemed extremely shy.

One day, about four weeks into rehearsal, after we'd been looking at and smiling at each other for several days, he came up to me and tapped me on the shoulder. I turned around. He did nothing.

"J.T.?" I said.

"I wrote somethin'," he said so no one would hear.

"Great!" I said. "You want to read it to the group?"

"No," he said quietly. "You first."

Rehearsal was over and he pulled out a crumpled piece of notebook paper on which sentences were scrawled and crossed out in ballpoint pen on each side.

He read to me in a halting monotone way, as if he hadn't had much education. But his sentences were clear and his descriptions vivid. He read about how much he'd wanted to be in this certain gang like the New York Bloods. They were powerful, owned big cars and stole TVs, stereos, DVDs and had a Mafia type fence to which they sold their goods. He saw that they were proud Latinos, they had knives and guns and were the unquestioned leaders in the 'hoods. He'd hung around them since he was a kid (he was fifteen at this point) and finally got up the guts to ask to join. This General liked J.T. so laid out an initiation plan for him. He had to burn a circle on his arm with a cigarette. Drink "a whole shitload of beer without getting sick," get a girl to have sex with him, spray paint a wall, just one crime after another. He got cheered on for his accomplishments, but he said in his writing that "something seemed kind of boring about it."

The final step of the initiation was that he had to pick a gang member from another area, take a knife and slash him clear across the face without getting caught. J.T. wrote in detail about buying the knife, and stalking the kid the general assigned him. He admitted he had doubts, but if he backed out they'd spread the word that he was a pussy. He read the last part very fast and he talked about getting the guy in Brooklyn under one of the subways and digging his knife in and pulling it down the guy's face. He said he hated it, especially when the guy screamed, but his guys were waiting for him and now he was an official gang member. He was wiping tears from his eyes as he read the last part, but I was still wondering whether I should turn him in to the cops. Physical violence was absolutely forbidden in any of my shows. Kids were immediately fired. Once a kid pulled a knife on me when I fired him and I said, "You can stab me but you're still fired."

I asked J.T. if he'd checked up on his victim and he said yes, the guy had to get all kinds of stitches and his guys had been looking for J.T. for months. He told me he thought gang life was "kind of ridiculous." "Everybody's got to be a *man*. I thought maybe I'd like to be in a TV series." He seemed guilty, scared and, now that he'd told me his story, younger and more helpless. I told him I wouldn't turn him in if he stayed away from gang life from then on. "Oh man," he said. "It's worse than death, looking over your shoulder all the time."

He read his story to the cast and they encouraged him to memorize it and do it in the show. Some of the guys laughed nervously. One girl was disgusted. "He'll be scarred for life," she said. But J.T. stayed and it turned out he could do a form of martial arts quite well so I had him teach it to the company. When it was free dancing, he did a tiny but sexy little salsa. I gave him some other scenes to be a part of in the show. He'd nod and get to work, but he never hugged or let any of us touch him like many of the other kids.

Then, one day, a week or so before we were leaving to perform the show at New York Stage and Film at Vassar, he didn't show up. I called the numbers he'd given me, but they were fake. I walked the Lower East Side and the way Upper East Side hoping to spot him or kids who might know him. It was hopeless. He was gone. We rearranged the show and another kid read J.T.'s monologue. I went over and over in my head what I'd missed or done wrong. There were signs. There must have been. The cast was quietly angry with me for not being able to keep this tough sweet complicated friend.

We went on. The show was great at Vassar and many of the kids got their first look at a college campus.

Three years later I was at the dog run at Houston and Mercer and I saw J.T. slowly walk up to the fence that protected the dogs from running into the street. He smiled and put his face against the fence.

"Come in," I said.

He shrugged. "No."

"How've you been?" I asked him.

"Okay. But I got out of jail a bunch of months ago. I'm looking for work. You doin' any shows?"

"Jail," I said.

"Car stuff," he lied. "I'm outta gangs though and doing the parole thing."

He had more scars on his hands.

I had nothing to say.

"That time with the theater thing," he said. "That was real." He tapped the fence and walked away.

"Please, don't fuck up!" I shouted after him. "You're worth a lot."

He smiled and did a karate chop in the air.

Deidre, Sean, and Shun, *The Red Sneaks* (1989)

I wanted to find a metaphor for addiction that wasn't clichéd or like a public service announcement. I had always been in love with Michael Powell and Emeric Pressburger's movie, *The Red Shoes* with Moira Shearer. Her Svengali-like relationship with her choreographer was enhanced by the magical shoes that kept her dancing and dancing to death.

I developed a piece called *The Red Sneaks* in tribute to that film and also because dancing was at the center of teenage energy. Hip-hop was starting to come in and teams of dancers were trying out combinations of acrobatics and dance that were funky and inventive. The spell of illegal drugs has never been broken and new drugs arrived on the scene it seemed like almost daily—ecstasy, crystal meth—but the real Satan of the time was crack. Such dope was the *Red Sneaks* for poor and rich kids alike.

I held conventional auditions for my show, which was produced by Theater for New Audiences and would be performed at the Perry Street Theater. But having "professional" kids come in and sing for me one at a time just wasn't for me. I don't know what it is to be a "professional" kid. The idea of kids going around to theaters pretending to be kids other than they are makes me sick. It's like preteen beauty pageants or all the pretend happiness in *Barney*.

Luckily I was walking through Prospect Park one day and I saw two kids dancing like wild but graceful animals. They leapt, they spun, they did great hip and shoulder moves. They stood on their heads and flipped from their feet to their hands. They had great laughs too. I sat down with them. One was Deidre and the other Sean. I think they went to Jefferson High. I don't remember, but it was a Brooklyn Public School. I asked them if they were practicing for a contest.

Deidre was a firecracker. "Hell, no," she said. "I dance because I dance. Because track team is over and I still gotta move!"

Sean was more reserved but he had a kind face and wise eyes. Deidre was wild but I could tell Sean's calm soothed her. I've never claimed to be psychic but after years of experience I am capable of identifying certain qualities in kids. These two both had a kind of deep kindness and empathy. They were clean and uninterested in trouble. Sean was studying like crazy to get into a New York State college and Deidre was Deidre as she chomped away at every bit of life she could get. She was definitely the girl with the red sneaks. Both of them were poor, but Sean had plans, two jobs and a touch of anger at his life. It disappeared as fast as it came and was replaced by a teasing quality and mischief. He would make an ideal Svengali, sorcerer, Satan (the character of the Pusher).

There was another boy in that very small group who interested and troubled me. He had a regular name but we called him Shun. Shun was very tall for fifteen and what could be accurately described as "cute." Girls in the audience inched their way up to him after shows to get a closer look and receive attention. I cast Shun as the sincere lover who wanted the girl to give back her sneakers and go off with him, but I might as well have made him the sorcerer. Shun was sweet and very smart and early on I could see he was his own man and a bit of a hustler. He didn't tell me, but he already had a manager and commercials and kids' shows planned. He never truly committed himself to the show. His eye was on what was next. Once he and Sean approached me and gently informed me that the two raps I had written for the show were really pretty pathetic. Gladly, I sent them off to start all over again and they found words and beats that were more appropriate for their age and the show. I was a little embarrassed, but thankful.

Diedre went on to do a fabulous high energy Red Sneaks girl and stayed with me another two years to help me write and play the lead in a play called *The New Americans* which dealt with parents who immigrated and couldn't adjust to American customs. Meanwhile the kids themselves were becoming more and more American despite the painful bullying they received at school. Deidre was fierce about this because she came from Trinidad. Then she shocked me by getting married and having babies, but the energy of her enthusiasm always uplifted me.

Sean's older brother was murdered in a drug-related feud. I went to the funeral in a tiny church in East Brooklyn. Sean was a changed kid. I was afraid his hidden anger would bust out and get revenge, but when I saw him much later, he was a student at Oswego in psychology.

Shun has been the lead in a very popular primetime sitcom for five or six years. I hear he has four children. I still have a tiny red high top sneaker the cast gave me for opening night.

Sosua John, *Sosua* (2010)

I do many shows that don't involve kids but every two years or so I have to go back into the fray. Recently I was approached to see if I would do a show on the odd but transformative story of how the Dominican Republic rescued eight hundred Jews from Hitler. The grant stipulated that only kids from Washington Heights could participate. So I had to find kids with a longing to learn about the worst cruelties man had ever experienced and yet simultaneously how the reaching out of an equally poor and persecuted people helped heal and keep more Jews from perishing.

His name was John and right away I knew he'd be the central force creatively as well as the kid who could keep a very disparate and difficult group together. In Washington Heights, Jews and Dominican people rarely mix.

John is such an exceptional kid that he seems too unreal to write about. His parents are from the Dominican Republic and, even after twenty years, speak barely a word of English. I asked John why and he shrugged. There was too much story to go into.

John lost his older brother to cancer three years ago and decided he had to set an example for his much younger brother whom he would guide and watch over. He had to get out of Washington Heights. So completely on his own he looked up a multitude of boarding schools where he could get a college oriented education and he'd be away from the drugs and hustle of his streets.

He was accepted by a boarding school near Princeton, New Jersey, on full scholarship and excelled academically. He also found he had a curiosity about theater. It so happened that the young drama instructor was a protégé of mine named Aaron Bogad. Aaron told John all about me and *The Violence Project,* of which he'd been a part.

Sosua, the show about the Jews and Dominicans, took place in a community center in John's Washington Heights neighborhood. When Aaron heard that John would have the opportunity to work with me he made a special program for the quiet brilliant seventeen-year-old and Aaron also contacted me. This was a rare and beautiful circle which would have meant nothing if John himself wasn't extraordinarily committed and made the commute from Princeton to Washington Heights two nights a week. He happened to be a very talented young actor and was always around to help move furniture, make props, clean up. Aaron continued to encourage John and I was proud of Aaron for the complicated work he'd obviously done with this kid.

Another coincidence in John's life was that he had decided to apply to NYU Tisch School of the Arts for acting. He applied early admission for a full scholarship. I was to write a recommendation letter for him partly because I teach full-time there, which I don't think he knew. This boy worked so hard, but the fates were also with him. He was accepted and is now a freshman at the Experimental Theater Wing where Aaron studied and I taught. He is also once again playing the lead in *Sosua* paying tribute to the kindness of his ancestors and setting the example he wishes for the skinny little boy who follows him around.

Bruce, *Runaways* (1979)

His hair was blond and messy. His eyes were light blue and so intense you almost couldn't look into them. He was always passionately searching, searching for anything he might miss. When I knew him he had the seriousness of a child who refused to be left out of anything. And there was a temper tantrum close to the surface ready to explode.

He was impatient because regular conversation seemed to go faster than signing and he had so many ideas, opinions, accusations and praises to get in. He was a beautiful boy all over who would give you unexpected bear hugs or would laugh happily for no reason.

I'd put the word out that I wanted to find a "deaf kid." I wasn't politically correct in those days. I wanted to have as many types of young people represented in *Runaways* as possible. When I was with Peter Brook we'd worked with the National Theater of the Deaf and I'd found the signing to be graceful, expressive music that I hadn't run into before.

I explained to Bruce that I wanted him to sign all the songs from within the group. There'd be no lady in the corner. His interpreter would be right by his side and if he acted well enough, the audience would forget she was there. And they did. He was a phenomenal actor. Because of his disability his whole body naturally expressed speech. Every inch of him reacted to what he couldn't hear, but would blast his own unique energy with all his senses.

The show was a dream for him. For once he was not just equal but special. For once the problems that held him back contributed to a positive beloved identity. He worked for hours with his interpreter to make every phrase like a dance with his hands. It was hard not to watch him. One on one he could read lips and was militant about keeping his interpreter away. He was easily frustrated with her although loving and patient with the younger kids. He taught them the alphabet and basic signs. The whole group was required to do the same.

When he did his "monologues" you could hear him grunting as he signed because he wanted to communicate so badly. He had the commitment that no one else in the troupe could duplicate. He *had* to be heard.

Once he asked me if he could stop signing and just sing and talk like everyone else. He knew the whole show in his mouth and body. I swallowed slowly and explained to him that I'd hired the young actors to be young, the Latinos to be Latino, the blacks black, and I needed their inner knowledge and identity. I *needed* him to sign. It was one of the main reasons he'd been hired. He was devastated. But no one would tell him that his voice came out sometimes like an out of tune groan.

After *Runaways* closed, he made it his mission to work with non-hearing actors to make great theater. He was only twenty but he was the most serious and recognized artist in his community. I'll never forget his intensity. As if his hands were grabbing at the air for every sound out there.

He died at thirty-four of AIDS. But he left many young actors behind who were not just proud, but gave off his unique style of romantic arrogance for what he was and the miracles he planned to do for himself.

Linda Mills, *The Reality Show* (2010)

I. Linda Mills

If a building fell on me and I had only one call I could make, I wouldn't call 911; I wouldn't call the fire department or the police. I would call Linda Mills—Vice Provost and Head of Student Affairs for New York University. The only danger would be that she'd be off somewhere on an obscure island in Indonesia filming a documentary, building a school and starting a fabric export company. Even so, she'd have the cranes and diggers and drills organized to rescue me faster than Mayor Bloomberg could do it, and she'd already have found the best hospital in New York City for people who've been crushed by buildings, and saved me the best doctor and a bed.

Linda Mills is one of my mentors and consigliere at NYU where I teach fulltime. I have never seen a woman juggle so many major life-changing decisions at once and still have time to have a husband and a son, to work out, to make a documentary about her mother who survived the Holocaust, and to manage to dress extremely tastefully, too. She has a temper, she has enough passion and heart for all four vice provosts, and she is the practical executor of the ideas of our wild visionary—President John Sexton.

About seven years ago, there were several suicides in a row at NYU. Linda, who is also a social worker, lawyer, and author, was terrified that the notion of suicide was becoming contagious and even attractive. She posted psychologists and teachers in every dorm to watch out for the kids and listen to any dangerous talk.

After that, she decided that there should be a program that would speak to the freshmen at NYU about issues they would face as they entered a fast moving competitive college in the middle of the most tempting, exciting, and potentially dangerous city in the USA. She enlisted Zoe Ragouzeos, Director of Health Promotion, Wellness Services and Emergency Response at NYU. At thirty-seven, Zoe is a prodigious, droll clinical social worker, who put together a hotline that kids could call when they were feeling confused, depressed, or suicidal. Then Linda and Zoe had to put together a program to "advertise" the hotline. Linda bought a packaged "know yourself and who you are" group that the kids thought was corny and close to useless.

So the next year, Linda called me into her office, probably because of my experience with *Runaways*, and asked me if I would devise a show for these naïve and somewhat fragile freshmen. I told her first and foremost that we had to cast the most talented undergraduates we could find and put on a show that was so good, so professional, and so committed that the freshmen would barely know we were feeding them the number to the hotline again and again and *again*. We needed a lot of humor. And dancing. And singing. Linda got my concept immediately, and took off to convince twenty or so other administrative people to spend a bit of money to put on the show. She and Zoe put together a list of controversial issues they wanted to cover including loss and emptiness, Internet addiction, domestic violence, drugs, alcohol, depression, and of course, suicide. Linda and Zoe and I are proud because we are in the sixth year of *The Reality Show*, which was performed at Radio City Music Hall this year. Because the cast members repeat the number of the hotline in many ways and ad nauseum, there are now up to nine thousand calls a year, and each call represents trouble averted.

Linda, while both ferocious and sharp as a knife, cries every year at *The Reality Show*, for she is also a softie. And the show, which has grown from a cast of eight to eighteen, has genuinely helped freshmen adjust to the spectacular but overwhelming experience that is NYU. I am proud to call Linda Mills my loving friend on top of it all and think everyone should have a Linda Mills. Linda Mills should have a Linda Mills. If she did, the world could change even faster.

II. *The Reality Show*

So *The Reality Show* gets its name from the fact that it deals with real life but it has nothing to do with the odd, gossipy tabloids on TV. It is done by and about young people facing the choices that confront them in college and the consequences of these choices, about the reality of being grown up enough to travel dangerous roads. This is not a goody-goody entertainment. *The Reality Show* has to dispense accurate information in a completely upfront way to get through to its audience.

I bring to the productions my belief that college students have more strength, power, and instinctive intelligence than adults who have been jaded by experience and habits. And that's why young people are so scary and wonderful. Look at rock 'n' roll. Next to firing off guns in a war or blowing up a building, where can we find a more destructive, loud, threatening sequence of noises? Only punk, heavy metal, alternative rock, and even good old Rolling Stones and Beatles, are incredibly threatening with their honesty. This potential for power is innate in most people from the age of seventeen through their early twenties. I think most people are afraid to think of what the young can do. But I treasure the danger, the energy, and the surprises.

I find a new rush of life every time I do a project with young people and they have seldom failed me. I think it's a fact that I get so renewed by them that I can't help but respond to their beauty. They feel my true admiration. Plus, I trust them. The ones I choose to work with are still open to all the possibilities of the world and rarely manipulate or cop attitudes that censor spontaneity. I also love their clothes. After four months watching them show up at rehearsal with tube tops, sparkling high tops, ripped and decorated jeans, jackets slashed down the middle, rubber band bracelets, combs, feathers, and chopsticks in their hair, T-shirts that read KISS A ZOMBIE or I AM NOT YOURS, I cannot stand going back into a world where fabrics match and the decibels are reasonable. Why don't adults roll around on the floor and practice flips and blow bubbles and share McDonalds fries by shoving them into each other's mouths? Why don't they bump their bottoms and wear tight clothes no matter what their weights or shapes? And why is it that, if most great popular music is created by kids in their teens and twenties, we don't give these same artists the opportunity to make theater.

The combination of this willingness of young talent and the support of an adult team is what makes *The Reality Show* what it is. Linda Mills and Zoe Ragouzeos teach the company about the depth of the problems they are portraying. In this way, we don't have the superficial tears or sulking of bad television. With the professional team behind the hardworking cast, we end up with theater that is more like a ritual, more like a genuine back-and-forth between audience and actors. For me, the exchange never gets boring. NYU is very open to letting us be courageous. There is no subject too sensitive to be in *The Reality Show* and I believe that the actors themselves get rid of some of the demons that have been riding on their own backs.

The first year, I auditioned up to three hundred kids in June to find my eight dramatic messengers. Then we rehearsed five days a week all summer. Now eighteen cast members devote July and August in the same way. I have seen remarkable moments of artistic bravery that I doubt could happen anywhere else. The young actors write, sing, and dance about depression, feeling lost and alone, being broke, sick, addicted to drugs, stupid with alcohol, pressured to the point of madness with work, competition with peers, feeling mediocre, feeling nothing, and much more. But they are funny. Really funny. I know that if the show isn't beautiful and hilarious, no one will care. And by the time each summer of rehearsal is over, the remarkable thing is that not only are the young actors skilled and funny, but they also care as much about helping the freshmen stay safe as they do about their own performances. It has happened every time so far.

One year, for sexually transmitted infections, we used puppets that were dressed like Chlamydia, Herpes, etc. This year we did a fashion show with a full boutique of costumes showing the same. One year, for showing pressure in academia, one of our more athletic members of the cast did a circus leap over three classmates who were reciting the pressures he was facing, then three more classmates came on and he managed to leap over like any professional gymnast and land without hurting himself. But when the pressure got to the point where the whole cast was lying down and he had to leap over them, he had to be stopped, even though he was willing to hurt himself to get the work done. To show all the problems that go on between roommates, there are two girls who come to the front of the stage. One has a horrific, ear-splitting laugh. The other describes what it is like to live with her. At the end of the routine, the terrorized roommate poisons the giggling girl. Then, of course, we have what we call Public Service Announcements where an actor comes forward and says, "If you're having problems with a roommate, arsenic is not the answer. Talk to your Resident Assistant." Another great example of using theater to express danger is when a young man brings out his violin and uses it to describe what it's like to complete a long and late essay using something like Adderall to keep him jazzed and awake. With twenty milligrams, it's doable—with forty, the violin goes insane, faster and faster and faster. The actors in the background are trying to follow him on their imaginary computers and everyone is "typing" at increasing speed. We use this to demonstrate the notion that you shouldn't abuse even prescription drugs. These are just four examples of the improvisations, stories, and sketches that I've seen my casts invent. I'm very lucky because they provide me with so much laughter, extraordinary music and tenderness. They are also, often, a pain in the ass. But that comes with the territory.

I am ashamed, when I see what is possible in the blossoming human character, that professionals in the arts often teach petty, competitive attitudes. When I set strong boundaries, strict rules, and mutual respect, I can end up with a crowd of what I call "young shamans." They heal and they mystify. Over the summer, their voices grow, their bodies get strong, and their energy doubles in stamina. Each individual contributes something unique to the whole, whether it is break dancing, beat boxing, gymnastics, dance, vocal sounds, brilliant comic sketches, slapstick, or bodywork. But strangely enough, by the time this arduous work is done, there is no one cast member who dominates. If I have done my work properly, they are a true ensemble. This is a concept that was developed and popular in the seventies and eighties but has been superseded more recently by the "superstar" era with the writer and movie star as king. Ensemble work is especially touching when you witness the generosity that emerges from what is a narcissistic time of life in these all-over-the-place, growing, hormone-colliding, identity-searching creatures.

Today, *The Reality Show* remains totally multicultural, very diverse in looks, character, and individual strengths. The cast has written it all and composed almost all of the songs (with some songs taken from last year's show). This year, Radio City Music Hall was filled to the rafters with freshmen who were thrilled, terrified, self-conscious, arrogant, pretending to know it all, but yes, innocent, and the cast gave them what I thought was a great performance. I also felt as though something that took place in that huge arena felt almost intimate. When *The Reality Show* works, it feels like more than just onstage entertainment. There is a reaching out, there is the passing on of crucial information, there is always the wish to give a kind of balm to the terrified freshmen and, of course, many suggestions of ways to experience the true buoyancy and unique, once-in-a-lifetime experience of college. And yet, it is a show. What that says to me is that theater can be something very magical. This year, as in every year so far, this performance is an occasion when I truly believe in the power and potential of theater. I appreciate the well of talent in so many people. I remember how a family can be made, and I am grateful for the moment of fate that connected me to such a truly transformative time for all of us.

IV. More Persons of Interest

Family Matters

Edward

My family was as full of artists and writers as it was of madmen. My mother's brother Uncle Edward lived on an island in Hawaii for years, took mysterious journeys where no one could find him, and returned to publish a book on an esoteric composer named Charles Griffiths. Then he'd go off somewhere and return when we least expected him. He was one of the first people to introduce Tai Chi to the American public. Again he published books, disappeared, returned, and became one of the first to bring the Alexander Technique into dancers' and actors' exercises. This teaching was a method for healing problems with posture and the spine and now is used everywhere. He was forty years ahead of our current culture. I don't have a clue where he went on his journeys, and I don't know where he gathered his knowledge about so many obscure subjects. He himself was physically an expert in these techniques. He was obviously an adventurer, but you'd never know it by looking at him. He was slender, hardly muscular, wore thick glasses, and really was the cliché of a nerd. He'd been brilliant at the violin but his father, who was a "son of a bitch tyrant," said "sissies play instruments" and pushed him toward sports. My Uncle Edward would be more likely to know the Greek name and origin of a game than how to play it. My mother adored him because he had a quirky bitchy sense of humor and never hesitated to eviscerate one of their sisters or my father if they were depressing her. The negative thing about Edward was that he had no follow through. You couldn't count on him to stick around or pay back the money he constantly borrowed from my other uncles. Edward was the most secretive member of my mother's family. He was always in debt. And yet his friends, from what I could discern, were high class. He was very close with all the members of the New York City Ballet, having introduced them to the Alexander Technique. He was friends with George Balanchine and a close companion to Balanchine's second, the woman who drilled the dancers in their rigorous warm-ups.

He always implied that she was his girlfriend, but my cousins and I speculated that Edward was gay. He talked in an affected kind of over-expressive way. He dropped names. He was obsessed by his sister's and niece's sense of fashion.

Edward was also our "beatnik" relative. He was the artist and the rebel. When I was in college he might call me up and ask me if I'd heard some country song that had "the wisdom of the sages." To everyone else he was "amazing" Uncle Edward. But I began to suspect that he was fiercely competitive and gossipy about the people (me included) who were getting more attention than he was.

Despite his secrecy with me, other cousins had a freer, more open access to his life. He and I lived in New York at the same time for years. We went to Indian and vegetarian restaurants to talk about poets and blues singers but, although he'd been to my various apartments and my loft, I'd never been invited to his. Still, since the early years of my life as a composer and writer were up and down with many people, I prefer to think of him as the hilarious closet queen from a straight middle class Buffalo, New York family who traveled the world and taught me about poets (he once sent me an epic poem out of the blue called "The Albatross" and I set the whole thing to music for a show). He also kept me current about new rock bands (though he was thirty years older) and bitched about my father and his conservative ways despite the fact that my father supported him most of the time.

My Uncle Edward knew about the Bhagavad Gita and the Koran. He practiced Sufism for a while though he often talked in Yiddish phrases when visiting Buffalo. What a strange man he was. But he's inside me. And, best of all, it was he who insisted that, when I was six or seven, he had to be the person who took me to see *The Nutcracker Suite* for the first time. We had the best seats in the house.

Another artistic member of my family was my second cousin Edmund. But he wasn't secretive. He was just fabulous. He was extremely tall, way over six feet. He had light brown wavy hair and Caribbean Ocean blue eyes. I thought he was the most gorgeous man living and when I was a little girl he used to lift me up and I felt as if I was looking at my living room from the top of the Empire State Building. He had a low smooth voice like the newscaster's on television. And, despite his size, he was gentle and in a state of wonder about life. Even at a very young age I could feel his love and curiosity about who I was and who I was going to be. When I was a teenager her encouraged me over and over to play him my songs, unlike Edward who, after a while, lost interest in my music completely.

Whereas many in my speedy neurotic family could make me feel invisible, Edmund made me feel (even at five-years-old) beautiful and important. I would always wake up early on the mornings I knew he was coming to visit and put on what I thought to be my most "artistic" outfit. My mother found this to be hilarious, but she did the same thing. There are many stories or rumors about my mother and Edmund during World War II while my father was overseas. It's said that my mother (who was twenty or twenty-one at the time) had poker games at the house with young men who were wounded or hadn't been drafted for one reason or another. They say she broiled steaks for the guys, poured beer, and played the favorite musical hits of the era. Edmund must have been fourteen or fifteen at the time, and sometimes my mother danced with him. He told me that once he got an erection and my mother just laughed good-naturedly and left him in the kitchen where he could calm down.

Edmund was always the best source of material about the mother I dreamed of having, but in reality she was too drunk or sick to be around much. He told me that she had had gorgeous wavy thick red hair and a lithe athletic body. He said she wrote beautiful poetry and would read aloud with a deep actress' voice. He said he accompanied her to the Vets hospital when she went to comfort the soldiers. In Edmund's eyes my mother had a tough and quick mouth and could beat anyone to a pun or a joke, but she was also extremely fragile and had terrors about my father and my brother Lincoln. Edmund put my mother on a pedestal, but was well aware of her problems. I know he was in love with her. She rarely spoke of him to me, but my father knew it too and didn't seem to mind.

Edmund was a filmmaker and an intelligent dreamy Harvard graduate. The family had its first real flash of fame when he won an Academy Award for best documentary. My mother stayed on the phone with him for an hour. I have a clear picture of her, a lovely joyous look on her face, a Scotch in one hand, a cigarette in her mouth. She praised him and joked with him and looked as sexy as he always made her feel. I also remember going through Times Square with the two of them; he bought me a ukulele from a pawn shop window. After that he took all the credit for my composing. He knew many famous actors and directors but didn't show them off. He and his second wife, Deni, lived on Central Park West, and every Thanksgiving I'd go up to get a first row view of the Macy's parade. I was taken aback by the notoriety of the other guests.

After my mother killed herself, Edmund was the only one who would really have an honest conversation with me about mental illness, my parents' marriage, and the act of suicide itself. He was a bit of a mystic by then but we wrote a screenplay together about four suburban housewives who secretly form a masked punk rock band together and become superstars. We couldn't sell it, but I loved sitting in the thick leather chair of his den, his long legs stretched across from me. We jabbered back and forth about what the characters would do, what kinds of songs, and sing in what kind of voices. Nothing happened to the script and I had a gig in Europe or at La Mama and we moved on. He was still writing and making documentaries when he died from a brain tumor.

Many people died when I was a young person, but at Edmund's memorial, I sobbed like I'd never done before. My father was shocked to see me grieving and weeping beside him. I think I was saying goodbye to one of the kindest and most supportive men I'd known. But, more than that, I was saying goodbye to a part of my mother that no one else would ever know—the wild, smart lover. A woman who loved life for a short time and wasn't beaten by it because this man made her into a movie star.

I don't know much about my father's brother. They've cut each other off in an old-style Russian feud many times, and then they only partially reconcile. I mention Kim because he is another mysterious character. A fine painter and set designer, he did the original sets for *Blues for Mr. Charlie* and *House of Blue Leaves*, and was a resident designer for *Playhouse 90,* a weekly live television drama. He was successful enough to make the leap to Hollywood where he became artistic director for the *Amityville Horrors*. The culturally erudite Kim believed he was a great artist who had been drastically misunderstood and ignored. This might be true. He was extremely dramatic. The first time I saw him he reminded me of Dracula. He was tall and thin, wore a cape, and had a real white streak down the middle of his black hair. Both he and my father spoke in resonant British voices and Kim breathed tragically on the intake between sentences, as if each pause was a terrible memory. Kim was a hypochondriac of the highest order. Since he was a painter, his back was ruined, his hands would go in and out of paralysis, and sometimes he couldn't walk if the palpitations in his head grew too severe. His divorce destroyed him emotionally and he didn't recover for years. I met his wife once. She looked like an aging 1940s' babe. I don't know how he lived. He never came to Buffalo. It was "poison" for him. He rarely had jobs. I know my father supported him from time to time and resented it like an injured Jewish martyr. My father always had mixed feelings about Kim. He wasn't sure about his brother's talent, and didn't understand why Kim was always poor. I think my father believed that if an artist didn't have money, he wasn't very good. And Kim always claimed to be suffering from an obscure disease that cut back his teaching or prevented him from hustling his art.

Now my father is ninety-one and Kim a few years younger. My father is somewhat mystified and pleased because Kim got a rather large commission to paint extremely realistic portraits of all the important leaders and generals of the Third Reich. Kim won't say more than that, but for the last several years he's been steeped in creating Goebbels, Eichmann, and the rest of the gang. He is more comfortable financially and my father went to visit and said that the portraits were "quite accurate." Does anyone remember that we're Jews? But if Kim is a true artist, something must move him about this subject matter. One other interesting fact is that my mother was seriously dating Kim before she went out with my father. But no one ever speaks of that and Kim has four or five Nazi generals to go before the commission runs out.

Lillian Swados

My grandmother was a concert pianist. My father has told me this with a slight tone of disdain, as if because she wasn't Vladimir Horowitz she didn't count. But she played in small recital halls and women's gatherings, and I remember once my father, in a softer mood, saying with pride that she was a *real* concert pianist and teacher. But he never spoke of her much because she went mad. It began with her warming herself in a heavy shawl by the empty fireplace in midsummer as she rocked back and forth mumbling to herself. Then she got violent. She locked my father and his father and Kim in their rooms and smashed up the kitchen, using pots and silverware as weapons and screaming that she was being raped. My uncle said she threw knives at him, but who knows if that was true.

The treatment for such severe mental illness in the 1950s was lobotomy. She quieted down. Some days she would play *Rhapsody in Blue* for hours at a time. Other times she'd sit on her Victorian-style porch and curse at the girls on their way to an elite prep school. They laughed about her and did imitations. My mother didn't let her in the house, afraid that madness was contagious. So I crept out to the cab they had hired to bring her to our driveway. I'd stick my hand in the open window.

"How doo doodle toodle doo?" she'd say to me. "May the angels in heaven bless you."

Henry Brant

He is revered now. And the classical music world considers him one of their most original voices. After his death, the Guggenheim Museum paid tribute to him by having his piece for eighty trombones, soprano and organ performed all up and down its circular white curves. There was a long article in the Arts Section of *The New York Times* as well as a big obituary. He would've laughed at this or maybe spit at the invisible tight asses who were being forced to recognize him. He also would've been serene because he believed that, when it came to the arts, you had to be famous or "a god" as he put it if you wanted to get your music played or your paintings hung. He was sorry he wasn't a billionaire so he could produce all the artistic works of his friends that he felt were misunderstood or ignored.

He was my mentor for three years and one of the most brilliant teachers I've ever had. He was also mad as a hatter (much like the Mad Hatter in *Alice*). He was a bit of a boozer and a man who dreamed of creating a kind of music that could be played and heard around the whole earth at the same time. He also adamantly believed that where music was played was as important as what it was or how many times it was played. I found myself up a tree, under a bridge, running up and down a staircase, in a generator room, in a stream or marching in and out of the caféteria while I played the instrument he assigned me. He wasn't a dilettante. For him, music was not just his existence but everyone else's too. He despised the one note "hums and oohs that went on for hours" but he was the most spiritual companion I've ever met.

My first encounter with him was in my freshman year at Bennington when he rushed into our classroom dressed in shorts, a trench coat and a baseball cap and furiously scribbled a series of equations on the blackboard. When he finished scribbling, he dashed out. I have figured out now that the numbers had to do with overtones or the circle of fifths but, at the time, I wanted to be a folksinger and a radical. I didn't have a clue about the mathematics of classical music. Despite his saying that I wrote "melodies that give you calories," Henry Brant became my first mentor. We shared a love of noise. For one composition class, I brought in a cardboard mailing tube that I yodeled through, accompanied by a gong I made from a large saw blade. The bright green eyes behind his thick glasses lit up and he pounded on one end of the mailing tube to get a dark drum sound and tapped delicately on one of the edges of the saw blade with a violin bow. An eerie squeak came out. "Multiple uses," he said. "Multiple uses."

He wasn't a hack and knew just as much history and technique as any other professor, but to make money, he orchestrated for the movie composer Alex North. "*Cleopatra* really killed me," he said. "All those pseudo-ancient squeaks and so many phony Middle Eastern strings. I suggested they use clay pots, timpani and ouds for more authentic sounds, but they wouldn't listen."

I mostly despised classical music with the exception of Bartok, Ravel, Penderecki, Xenakis and Bach. I was moved by anyone who used choruses in a dramatic way or told stories; I loved playing around with my voice, imitating animals and construction sites. I wrote scenes for myself like a half-bird, half-woman who was trying to find a true identity. This pleased Henry because his spatial music was perfect for theater. "One day," he said to me. "I'm going to put orchestras on all the mountains surrounding Bennington and give each conductor a walkie-talkie. I'll conduct the whole thing from a hot air balloon." He didn't think about who'd hear it. He had the priorities of a real artist. He did his music his way. But he could also be bitter. "He's conducting himself. You're supposed to lead the orchestra like it's a battle—that's your job." He taught me how to conduct with simplicity and precision. And how to get the most out of each instrument. He used sounds like "bans titter kachung grrr and e, e, e," rather than conventional classical terms. I don't know if instruments were alive to him, but the world he made with thirty cellos, sixteen trombones and a tuba was a landscape. And when he did a solo concert mastering fifteen instruments, running from one to another, he was a musical athlete combined with a vaudeville comic. He was pleased with my passion for ethnic music (I commuted to Wesleyan to learn South Indian singing and African drumming). He liked the way I incorporated world sounds into noise and conventional harmony for Bennington drama projects. He could also be rigid and cold. I worked six months on an overture that was meant to sound like the Balinese Monkey Chant combined with sensitive electric drums and Celtic wailing. But when I brought it to him, he took one look at it and immediately handed it back to me. "You did it in ink," he growled. "First drafts are always in pencil." He'd barely speak to me until I recopied my work. When I brought it back, he sat with me for hours and helped rearrange instruments and write melody lines in the right keys for the right instruments. He also arranged the Bennington Spring Concert with members of the Vermont Symphony Orchestra to play my piece. "It's real work," he said. "It deserves to be heard." He missed the premiere, however, because he'd gone out to dinner with one of his female colleagues and drunk too much. When he marched late into the concert hall he yelled, "Play it again! Play it again!" But there was no time on the program.

Henry's own career could be a mess too. He didn't have the prestigious commissions he wanted. When he got a job he procrastinated until things were on the verge of being too late to be performed. This could ruin his already controversial reputation. I can remember two or three times when six or seven of his most loyal students would stay up all night copying parts for the separate instruments that would come together to blossom into a symphony. Henry would stumble from one of us to the other checking out our work. He believed in precise penmanship and beautiful accents and dynamics. He never missed a mistake and made us copy over a page if it wasn't neat enough. He'd finish a section of the full conductor's score and then pass it on to us to divide and copy. His wife, who cooked by banging pots in the kitchen, and spoke like an exhausted Colleen Dewhurst, would serve us lemonade from time to time or scream at Henry to answer the phone. We all smoked weed when Henry wasn't in the room and giggled hysterically that we were a brilliant tyrant's little elves. Henry didn't miss a deadline while I knew him but the dissonant and dramatic aspects of his work often got scathing reviews. He was way before his time.

He told me that I was finding aspects of the voices that he'd never dreamed of and often had me sing my "bird" or "water" compositions for his buddies, the college bassoon and voice teachers with whom he often drank and improvised. When I left college early to join Ellen Stewart and La Mama he came to my rehearsal in New York to make sure I was following a "serious" career of music. He despised my folk and rock songs. But when I was hired to do the choruses for an experimental version of *Medea*, he followed my every step and discussed my choices with me. We had no money, so my orchestrations consisted of one broken triangle, a concert bass, guitar, saw blades, a bowed saw, a Tibetan drum and, of course, six voices chanting in ancient Latin and Greek. He infuriated Ellen because the show was to be done in a very dark basement with only candles and an occasional torch. She couldn't figure out who this little man in the baseball cap and trench coat was who insisted on using a penlight and taking notes. Henry was just as stubborn as Ellen because he did not want her ideas to force me into setting sloppy sonnets or to write "elevator music" melodies. Eventually they came to an amicable standoff, and Henry helped me receive my degree from Bennington without finishing my senior year, allowing my work in New York to count as school credits.

Medea won me considerable acclaim and Henry had me over to his apartment on the Upper West Side to celebrate. Then he asked if I would perform the lead vocal part in a piece of his that was to be premiered at Carnegie Hall. I was stunned. I was anything but Renée Fleming. Then I saw that the part was perfect for me. There was to be a full orchestra onstage—somewhat dark in mood, stodgy, disapproving. And then in the balcony there would be a high school marching band, free, young and rebellious. I was to be a bird that screeched between the two of them trying to negotiate a kind of peace. Henry had written this one- or two-minute solo for me. I knew I was not the only student that he nagged, aggravated, tortured and went far out of his way to develop and give great chances. He was as loyal as he was manic and as gifted as he was chaotic. I'll never forget standing in the balcony of Carnegie Hall with some New Jersey marching band screeching in a cornucopia of sounds as the audience looked up at me and laughed. What a debut! What great theater.

The last time I saw him was on his eightieth birthday. He was a bit tipsy but gave me a big hug. "I have a great idea for us," he said. "Let's make a silent movie and then we'll score the hell out of it." "I don't know how to make a movie," I said to him. He shrugged. "I guess you'll have to learn."

Peter Brook

No one can keep a silence longer than Peter Brook. Except of course a dead person and the corpse would squeak before Peter would blink. Peter Brook has been called a genius and an eccentric egomaniac. If you were lucky enough to see his work with Shakespeare when he was a young man, there would be no question as to his vast knowledge and originality. I believe Peter Brook is an adventurer and explorer. He directed a production of *A Midsummer Night's Dream* that was designed completely in white. He used trapezes and carousels. He collaborated with his composer, Richard Peaslee, to actually invent a plastic tube that, when spun around, made an eerie but childlike, breathing whistle. The production was one of the most famous Shakespearean interpretations there has ever been and it opened doors for hundreds of productions afterwards that reinvented and freely interpreted the world of the sacred Bard.

Peter Brook may have been hesitant to admit he was an upper class Jew because he was determined to make theater for all people. He had an overpowering dream of making a world theater where all cultures could come together and find a universal language of sounds and gestures. When he'd had enough of Shakespeare, he picked up his family, moved to Paris and began to create his global dream. Then he traveled extensively to find the actors who had the breadth and spontaneity to work towards new forms.

I was not a part of the company the first year, but when I was in Paris with Ellen Stewart, she told me she was going to "have a talk with Mr. Brook." I had no idea who he was. He was a full-fledged La Mama "baby," but I still wasn't that interested in theater and had no idea who this prim yet mischievous half-bald man was who kept staring at me. Then I found out that he was the force behind staging *Marat/Sade*, the only play I'd seen that, to me, wasn't theater at all. It was a total experience of the senses and mind and the emotions. It took place in an insane asylum and the story was that the inmates were putting on a play for the authorities and royalty to demonstrate how safe and clean the asylum was. The story the inmates performed was about the murder of the revolutionary Jean-Paul Marat, "directed" by the Marquis de Sade. The actors dressed in grays and were dusty and performed on a dirty floor that surrounded one piece of a set—the bathtub in which Marat was lying. The actors had spent months studying the actions and intentions of seriously insane mental patients. The play was also a political protest against the rich using artists as pets to perform when they pleased. A classic scene was when Glenda Jackson, playing a patient with sleeping sickness, roused herself enough to whip the dying Marat with her long straight dark hair. Other images were equally as bizarre and sexual and broke many barriers of the theater's classic "fourth wall," which means it involved the audience in a way that was chillingly close.

But Peter Brook was not interested in plays anymore and, even so, I was not much interested in him. I still held fast to the fantasy of becoming another Joan Baez or Odetta (only more theatrical and rock 'n' roll). The problem was that I didn't have the voice or the songs yet. But then Ellen told me that "Mr. Brook is taking his troupe to Africa," and a free trip to Africa was more than I'd ever dreamed of. I had one four-hour meeting with Peter Brook and I was totally taken in by his passion for one theatrical world, a passion that preceded the rest of the arts' interest by at least twenty years. He told me he wanted me to experiment with sounds, melodies and rhythm from all over the earth and to work with his actors so they could find a new way of singing. We'd spend three or four months in Paris preparing improvisational techniques and choruses that we could do on one simple carpet throughout Africa. No sets. I was terrified but inspired, and I remember that, even in our initial talk, he would lapse into those long silences. Since I was only twenty, I fidgeted, blushed, sweated, tried to talk, but the mysterious silence prevailed until he'd say something. "We don't want tunes from the radio or recordings," he said. "We don't want to imitate any automatic habits that have built up in our listening or singing. We have to research and find music that is sung from a place of absolute necessity and truth, redefining beauty, and learn to create our own rituals."

I went to Amsterdam and bought every drum, flute and stringed instrument from Appalachia to Nigeria to the Pygmies of the Ituri Forest.

I returned to Paris and met a theater troupe made up of a Japanese Noh actor, a black German cabaret singer, a French movie star, a leading actress from the Royal Court in London, an Indian Kathakali dancer, an African singer and dancer, a six-foot American female rock singer and an even taller towheaded man who was skinny, elastic and barely walked. There were others too, but these were the main players. Peter's wife, Natasha, a dark beauty of Russian heritage, was also part of the troupe. She had been a well-known Shakespearean actor. And there was the fascinating young Helen Mirren who was half brilliant curious actress and half soft porn star. She was fearless, unpredictable and scary. Since I was nearly ten years younger than most of the group, it didn't sit well with them that I was leading vocal exercises and rhythmic chants and drumming. But Peter left me with them and told me to give them a "general sense of musicality." I trudged on.

As our trip to Africa has been well documented in John Heilpern's book *The Conference of the Birds*, there's not much for me to add. But nonetheless there are some experiences that haunt me in both delicious and frightening ways.

There has been nothing in my life like crossing the Sahara Desert. Peter hired a team with jeeps and guides and supplies . . . we slept outside. Every day we got up in the freezing dawn and exercised and exercised to get our cold limbs going. We'd have breakfast and then drive and drive, through the lush sand dunes or the gravel or whatever texture the desert held out for us. I remember that in one oasis the buildings were all the color of sand and you almost couldn't distinguish them from the sand. The tiny place was a strict Muslim community. The whole town square was a mosque and the men wore these blinding white robes and scarves around their heads. The women were entirely covered in black. They wore burkas with only a small window around the eyes so they could breathe and see. Peter was trying to negotiate to see if we could do performances with them.

I caught the eyes of one of the completely covered up women. She signaled to me with the slightest gestures of her head and I took off after her in my combat boots and fashionable military pants and jacket and followed her around winding stairways that seemed to never end. After what seemed like a long time, she stopped in front of an immaculately clean white round house. Suddenly she pulled off her burka and I could see that she was a teenager—no older than fifteen or sixteen years old. She was wearing a T-shirt and jeans and had long dark hair and beautiful wide eyes that were lined with kohl. She waved at me then quickly put on her robe again. But for one moment we were two teenagers in the middle of the Sahara sharing a secret. Probably not so different from each other in some ways and worlds apart in others. When I told Peter of my encounter he smiled and his blue eyes shined, though he was fatigued. "You must treasure that," he said. "Who knows what was in that gift?"

I also found a nomad, a Tuareg, in colorfully dyed leather and piles of gray cloth and leather around his face. This was further on in the Sahara and we had stopped to take a break. I heard the sound of a flute coming from behind a bush and there was a young man playing around on a metal pipe with a hole drilled in it. He'd made a flute. His face was very angular, skin dark but not black, and he was folded up in the most complex position with his legs wrapped around each other. His breathy melody was melancholy and he stopped when he saw me. "No, go on," I said to him. "I like it so much." But he shook his long face and pointed to his chest. "Asthma," he said, coughed and turned his back to me.

Then there was the time when I got into a fistfight with the twelve-year-old Vestal Virgin of the Oshogbo forest outside Ife, Nigeria. I'd gone there just before dawn, wrapped in an indigo cotton cloth, so I could examine the holy statues and receive some individual spiritual attention. The Virgin, whom I'd seen the night before carrying the calabash in the sacred parade, was also in charge of guarding the forest. The forest was ancient. It was devoted to praising Shango, Oshun, and other of the Yoruba gods, all of whom had specific personalities and specialties such as music, crafts, planting, dance, and thunder. I thought I deserved a god. I wanted a religion of my own. I heard voices. I sang in tongues. I could hear each voice of the multilayered drums which pounded their ancestral poems into the night. No one was going to make me settle for a tourist's guided journey of the forest. I knew it would end up with the director of our theater coveting the real adventure and stealing ideas from the priest-guides. His wide-eyed obedient actors, with their beads and iron crosses, would follow behind, questioning neither what secrets they were missing nor why they were less deserving than he. Therefore, hours before the tour was scheduled, I crawled and leaped several miles in the dark, unafraid, until I reached the Forbidden Gate.

The Virgin popped out of the branches and leaves like an imp who lived inside the fat, twisted trees. "No," she said, "no, no," and I smiled as if it were a game. Here was a harmless little girl who stood between me and spiritual revelation. "I want to go in," I said cheerfully. "No," she said. Her hair was braided with dry leaves. She shook her head back and forth. "No, no, no!"

My mood began to shift just a little. I measured her holiness potential against mine. What gave her the right to refuse me my pilgrimage? Had she been born with a gift or attained her position through nothing but family connections? Surely, if she had sight, she would know I was a seer, too. Her face was painted with dry, dusty mud. Her heavy lids revealed expressionless eyes.

"I'm not going to *do* anything," I said, not knowing if she understood. "I just want to walk in the forest." She picked up a large branch and pointed it at me.

"White girl," she hissed. "White girl give me money."

"Phony," I spit at her. "Phony, phony. What kind of Vestal Virgin takes bribes?"

She continued to menace me with the stick. Now her eyes looked mad. The whites showed. The brown began to disappear. She hissed. Easy trick, I thought.

"White girl, give me money," she growled.

Now I was really angry.

"White girl!" I screeched. "White girl, white girl, *you* give *me* money!"

The calabash princess smiled, but there was no mirth in her expression. "White girl, give me money," she chanted. "Money, give me money."

I thought about the strange holy statues behind the gates. I pictured the dawn's light coming up over the jungle trees. I heard the rush of the purifying waters of the sacred river. I was furious. I wanted to go in. I grabbed at the little girl's stick and the two of us pulled each other's weight like samurai.

"Give me money, you little bitch," I shouted at her. "Fuck you and give *me* money."

"White girl, white girl, white girl," the little girl chanted. "You give me money, white girl."

The Vestal Virgin dropped the stick and starting punching at my shoulders. I threw the stick aside in fury and started slugging her in the face. She tried to claw my eyes and I stomped on her hard little feet. We fell to the ground and she dug her sharp little nails into my back. I was covered with leaves and mud. I became afraid. She was a tiny girl. What if I killed her? She was beating my rib cage until I thought it would break. Our hands still clung at each other's hair, but I managed to pry myself free. I backed off and tried to walk proudly on the dusty road toward my campsite. Contrary to what I expected, she didn't laugh at my departure. I turned slightly and saw her crawl, like a raccoon, up into the thick branches of the tree from which she'd appeared. Its leaves were rubbery and fat. The branches twisted like folded arms. She disappeared, protected from sight, even in the bright beams of the early-morning sun.

Africa changed my life and my whole way of perceiving music and dance and drama, from the idea of simple entertainment to comedic tragedy. Peter wanted us to communicate with each other on an individual or a deep spiritual level, like jazz, without words. Sometimes we would perform for villages and if we were doing an improv around something as simple as a pair of shoes or a bunch of wooden boxes, great comedy could take place, or weird indecipherable stories. Sometimes our work hooked right into the African sensibility and audiences went wild. Sometimes we failed miserably and ended up performing for a bunch of kids who were just looking for leftovers to eat.

Peter was very moody on the trips. Sometimes he'd be buoyant and pleased and we were allowed to follow giraffes in our Land Rover or share an outdoor grilled sheep at a festival for a subject we couldn't understand. But on other days we'd sit in a circle near the Land Rovers and he'd lecture us for four or five hours on what commitment meant, on how seriously we must take our exchanges with the Africans. He'd talk and talk until I couldn't understand what he was saying anymore.

And then there would be those silences. We'd have to sit and wait for him to gather the theatrical practical mystical thoughts.

Peter didn't believe that theater was merely a source of entertainment. He saw it as a way of life. All decisions and relationships reflected on what kind of artist you were. He, too, as a human being, stubborn and arrogant, was nonetheless willing to question himself. The Sahara and West Africa was the place to do it. He saw that I was struggling, too. At moments I thought I was truly in contact with gods and spirits who would lead me toward a truthful artistic voice. But other times I felt like we were a bunch of rich voyeurs trying to see how much we could steal from the tribes with whom we said we wanted a commonality. Peter and I shared a special vitamin water and drank it together every morning. He was considering sending me home because some nights I would howl and sing at the stars above the dunes. I weighed ninety pounds. But he let me stay because he knew I would learn and transform through the experience. And he was right. To this day there isn't an image or decision that isn't somehow informed by Africa and Peter Brook so long ago. He was a mysterious and infuriating mentor and teacher. He was also a brilliant scroll of all theater from all times.

My two years with him changed everything I believed about theater and art. He believed in finding the truth in gestures, in sound and the whole body's movement. He wanted us to rid ourselves of the years and clichés that had been instilled in us by bad theater, television and corrupt advertisements and politicians. He wanted us to learn how to reawaken our senses and used the phrase, "the beginner's mind." Could we make our art happen every time as if it was the first time? Peter's quest reminded me of the section from T.S. Eliot's *Four Quartets*:

We shall not cease from exploration
and at the end of all of our exploring
will be to arrive where we started and
know the place for the first time.

Peter Brook will always be an explorer and I learned to try to be a trailblazer from him.

Joseph Papp

After the considerable dose of global, somewhat avant garde, spiritually oriented music and theater, I was ravenous for the U.S., folk and rock 'n' roll. I'd had enough of mysterious wise infuriating men and somehow found a producer who was almost their exact opposite. Joseph Papp believed in the classics and Shakespeare—he founded Shakespeare in the Park at the Delacorte. But, more importantly to me, he produced hard-hitting political theater and encouraged young writers with original ideas. He was responsible for *Hair* and David Rabe's scathing Vietnam trilogy.

Papp's personality was also the opposite of the mentors I'd had previously. He was warm and tempestuous; he loved to make puns. He had a strong connection to his Jewish past, when he worked with his father selling clothes off a pushcart on the Lower East Side. Joe was direct, and although he too could talk a lot, he was an utterly different kind of dreamer. Ideas popped from his head like Athena from Zeus.

I invited Joe's wife and partner, Gail, over to my apartment and sang an hour's worth of my original songs to her. A lot of them were related to my dream of a musical of *Alice in Wonderland*. I wanted to do it like a Brazilian Carnival with each character singing in a completely different style of music and the variety of worlds defined by Lewis Carroll's words and sound—not costumes and dancing. Gail liked what she heard and passed her interest on to Joe.

After many months, Joe called me into his office and asked me if I wanted to do my *Alice*. But I'd been doing workshops in tough neighborhoods and jamming with musicians all over New York. I knew that the ideal image of the American family was full of holes and lies. There were more runaways populating the streets of New York than ever before and young girls were being picked up at Port Authority, drugged and turned out by dangerous pimps. Homeless teenagers were living in tenements and under bridges and there was more teen pregnancy, illness, gangs, violence and deaths than ever before.

I told Joe I wanted to do a show about these kids and *with* some of them too. I asked for a loft and enough money to pay twenty kids so we could train in dance and music and I could write a show based on the words presented and stories of the kids. He immediately said yes. "Okay, Swados," he said, "just don't burn down the building." I was stunned. I spent several months collecting a tough but talented and challenging cast and we began the process that ended up being the Broadway show *Runaways*.

Joe and Gail were equally supportive through the rollercoaster of that experience. We got tutors so the kids could stay all day with me. Joe bought lights for one school that was giving us a hard time about casting their student. Joe paid for a new set of pipes when, in the middle of winter, a whole system blew in the tiny apartment of our eighteen-year-old single father. Joe was charming, streetwise, threatening, sympathetic or simply direct with the principals, teachers and, above all, the parents he had to deal with. And they ranged from white to black, Hispanic, and Asian. Some were suspicious, arrogant or pushy. Without him I couldn't have kept my cast together.

Gail and Joe worked very hard with me on my lyrics and monologues. They both felt I had potential as a writer as well as a composer. I was so relieved to be treated as an artist in my own right, I worked twelve to eighteen hours a day, long after the kids went home. Joe and Gail and I became very close. When Joe didn't like the direction I was going in, he'd try to make me change it. I'd try his suggestion for a rewrite and, if it worked, I kept it. But I rarely did. I knew these kids better than he did and I'd examine the character of my junkie or child prostitute and find a solution that I knew was right for me. I fought him. Sometimes I won. Sometimes he did. Joe taught me to be clear and passionate in my writing. His faith in me, as with many of his writers, allowed me to take more risks. Sometimes we'd fight. It was very polite and cold. But if I created a moment that solved the problems, the ice would melt and we'd go to a Japanese restaurant.

The work on *Runaways* lasted two years. The phenomenal success of the show was as scary to me as it was to the kids. Joe didn't infantilize me but he knew that in some ways I was just as much a runaway as my cast members were. He and Gail, over the many years that followed, would take me to their country home in Katonah. Joe would blast Hasidic music on the cassette player and I'd go out to the porch and lie on their wide hammock. Sometimes Gail would come out and she'd talk to me about the plants and herbs in her garden, what and who inherited the land around the area and the history of that part of New York. Gail Merrifield knew more about so many things than most professors. And if she didn't feel that she was educated enough about a subject, she'd go out and find books, photos, pamphlets and completely educate herself on the subject. She was also very active politically on many issues. I don't know how many people knew this side of these two people, but Joe and Gail nurtured me, made me do research, try new foods and go on ridiculously long walks. They never stopped. They rarely rested.

I worked at the Public Theater on and off for eight years. I did productions that were successful and many that flopped. I wasn't a favorite of the critics, but Joe and Gail believed in my attempts to create new forms for musical theater. And this world was my home until the day Joe died.

We did end up doing my version of *Alice* and we cast pre-megastar Meryl Streep in the role of Alice. We rarely talked about the show or the character. I just told her that I did not want Alice to be a clichéd goody-goody little girl, that six- and seven-year-olds were full of mischief and curiosity. Meryl was also concerned that she couldn't sing (a fact she's disproved a hundred times since then). I asked her what kind of music she'd like to sing and she said Purcell. So I rushed home and wrote a new opening tune for her that sounded like bells and she sang it sweetly with a pure childlike soprano.

It was fascinating to watch her work because I don't think anyone had to give her a direction from that moment on. She just showed up one day in a pair of lilac overalls and green boots, and as the rabbit sang his samba, the caterpillar his raga and the Cheshire Cat his scat, she found her way into each scene and acted exactly like a six- or seven-year-old girl. She related to each character with hilarious curiosity, foot-stomping temper tantrums, tender rhymes and real openhearted joy. Meryl was not reactive as most Alices are. It was her show. She was not a temperamental artist, but she made sure she got what she wanted.

She did it by making a simple sound, "mmm" and then she'd ignore a suggestion and do what she wanted. But you couldn't get mad at her because she was a stubborn six- or seven-year-old little girl. And usually her choices were dead on. She was very kind and nurturing to me and asked intelligent questions about the performance of the music. I'd show her the answer, she'd pick it up quickly and she seemed to get over her fear of singing. Two mind-blowing scenes she did were at the end of Act One when the Red Queen holds a trial on whether to execute Alice or not and Meryl played every single character at the trial. She went at jet speed as she changed characters and voices and moods. It was a genius one-woman opera, but it never made it from the workshop Christmas show to the off-Broadway production. "Mmmm," I asked why. But I never got an answer. Another great moment was when Meryl decided to take on being both the White Queen and Alice in that scene full of whimsy and sadness from *Through the Looking Glass*. Meryl just decided one day to do it, and, of course, blew everyone's minds. It changed the scene to something completely else. I don't know. A mad monologue. A Beckett-like scene where the dialogue is going on in a different sphere. Or, of course, a six- or seven-year-old girl who is in wonder at a forgetful backwards lady that she might one day be. There was no question that Meryl's choice to do both roles was brilliant.

One thing that Meryl and I shared was a special love for Joe. It came from different places, different times and experiences, but we were both two people in his universe who wouldn't betray him. I remember seeing Meryl at Joe's funeral and sharing a moment that mirrored that similar special tenderness. Of course, she has rocketed into stardom beyond my comprehension. But I believe in her gifts and I believe in the life she has devoted to her transcendent art. I just miss the little girl in the lilac overalls (and was it green cowboy boots?). May she never go away.

Many years and many shows later, Joe took me out to Katonah. He wanted to talk to me. He told me about his illness and that his time was limited. He was in pain and not at his most eloquent. But he was a brave man and despite his scrappy, pugnacious reputation he had his dignity. And his dreams, too. A month later, I was sitting in a large office space with the designer Robin Wagner and Joe was planning a spectacle of a production based on the life of Marco Polo. He would bring some actors, he told me, but I'd have to teach Chinese actors the choruses. The assignment sounded impossible, but my hope soared. When were we leaving?

I don't think I did a piece of theater for at least a year after Joe died. It just couldn't be fun. It just couldn't be audacious. It just couldn't be a challenge beyond what I thought I could do. I recovered and have done more shows, oratorios and books over the years. I wonder what he would think of it all. There's some of my work that I believe has grown way past anything I did at the time. One would hope so. But I'll never have as great a home as I did at that Public Theater again. And there is absolutely no one producing in the theater who measures up to the generosity, spine and daring of Joseph Papp.

Yehuda Amichai

One beautiful and intense relationship I made was with the Israeli poet Yehuda Amichai. During a quiet hour I walked through the poetry section of a bookstore and saw a volume called *Amen*. The poems were by Amichai and translated by Ted Hughes. I opened to a section of the book and read:

Mr. Beringer, whose son
fell by the Canal, which
was dug by strangers
for ships to pass through the desert,
is passing me at the Jaffa gate;
He has become very thin; has lost
his son's weight.
Therefore he is floating lightly
through the alleys
getting entangled in my heart
like driftwood.

The phrase "He has become very thin/has lost his son's weight" went through me like a shock.

Simple. Lucid. Perfect. I thumbed through the rest of the book and came upon phrase after phrase that moved me, and challenged me, and filled me with an excitement I only felt when music was building inside me. I bought the book, took a cab home, and sat with my guitar for hours, leaning over Amichai's poetry. As always when I set a piece to music, I was engulfed by its images, and its rhythms took me over, so I was singing them over and over, as if I was writing the poem all over again. I don't remember how many hours I sat in front of *Amen*. I must've sat with my guitar for hours. Yehuda Amichai began to restore my soul.

I finally got to meet the man whose poetry I so adored. Yehuda was much older than me and had a worn face, as if it was made out of dust and clay. His eyes were sad, but he had a smile that often twisted slightly, as if he was thinking of a joke that he'd decided to keep to himself. The smile often broadened because he found much of what he saw in day-to-day Israeli and American politics amusing or absurd. He wasn't a handsome man, but nonetheless, very sexy.

I was nervous to sing the settings of *Amen* to him because it was clear that he had strong opinions and he didn't hide them. But he was very moved, and began pointing out other poems of his that might make good songs. His remote stare turned warm, and almost peaceful. We talked for a long time about poetry and people. He was a great gossip, especially about American literary figures and "great writers."

Eventually Yehuda and I made small tours around Israel. I'd sing his poetry in English, and he'd say it in Hebrew. Audiences found the evening very moving, and later on we booked reading/concerts in some cities in the USA. We called it "The Yehuda and Liz Show."

As a thank you for my music, Yehuda took me around the old city of Jerusalem on his own private tour. And no one knew the city better than he did. We walked and walked. It was like living inside one of his poems. I saw the sellers who sat outside the gates, as well as the Jewish section with the Tower of David and the Wailing Wall. He took me down into the Holy Sepulchre, where the Christian faithful lined up to see, as Yehuda called it, "Jesus' underwear." It was both striking and like a Fellini movie to see the colors of Roman Catholic priests, Russian Orthodox priests, all manners of nuns and tourists, all lined up in a very neat traffic pattern to take in the different sights. The Jews were no less comical, varied, and moving on the ancient streets, rushing from place to place. We went into the market, and I looked into the eyes of large dead salmon lying on ice.

Then we went to Yehuda's favorite place—a tiny café built on a Roman ruin, simple and completely without tourists, where boys with *pais* and Arabic kids played video games together noisily in the back of the tiled rooms. The tables were small and the ceiling was low, but Yehuda obviously felt a sense of history in that space. He was the most relaxed, almost peaceful, in that café, and said he often came there to write. While we were sitting, the Call to Prayer crackled over the loudspeaker, and the Arabs laid down their rugs to pray. The sound of the video games, the muezzins' voices over the airwaves, the Jewish sellers pitching prices and the quality of their goods were happening all at the same time. It was a kind of ecumenical Charles Ives concert, and I loved it.

The final stop on Yehuda's tour was located on the rooftops of a whole section of the old city. This was where the Ethiopians lived. It was like a miniature city with caves and windows dug into stucco and clay. The religious Ethiopians lived there, and I could see women grinding coffee, as well as tall, dark-skinned men herding sheep and goats. It was surreal. And yet Yehuda was delighted with my reaction. We took many such walks each time I came to Israel.

In honor of his sixtieth birthday, I wrote an oratorio musicalizing the sounds and pictures of Yehuda's magical tour. I received a Ford Foundation grant, and went searching around New York, its boroughs and suburbs, for Ethiopians, Russian and Greek Orthodox deacons, Roman Catholic priests, Ashkenazi and Sephardic cantors, as well as Yiddish, Shiite, and Sunni Muslim singers. I had to find people who were the real thing—who could sing their music legitimately, but who were not so religious and rigid that they wouldn't sing with each other.

At first, the "cast members" were highly suspicious of each other. They told stories of their people, and what had been done to them in the name of belief. There was an Armenian opera singer who spoke of the demise of her people. There was a Turkish Sephardic singer who spoke about the history of the Spanish Inquisition. The Ethiopian priest spoke of the persecution against his people, as well as did the Ethiopian Jew. There was an ex-Israeli Special Forces soldier, who spoke out against the Arab terrorists, and an Iranian Muslim who countered with anger that all Muslims were stereotyped and condemned. Each member of the cast was a magnificent singer, and many were experts in the liturgies of their sects. After all the talking and the tension, I asked them each to sing a lullaby from their country. As each religious singer heard the others' exquisite voices and tenderness in the modes for children, a peacefulness settled around the room. Many of the modes came very close to each other, and we could hear the similarities in melodies and vocal technique.

I made the oratorio out of these opposing harmonizing voices and used Yehuda's poetry to bridge them together. Over a period of three years, we performed at La Mama, Lincoln Center Out of Doors, an Italian Opera House, in the Old City of Jerusalem, and the Delacorte Theater in Central Park.

Yehuda and I stayed friends for many years, sharing a special kind of love that was neither romantic nor pompously "artistic" but, like his poetry, very deep and simple at the same time. When he died, I believed the world had lost one of its great poetic voices. He should have gotten more recognition as a great world poet. Maybe the fact that he was Israeli got in the way.

A Moment in LA in the Eighties: Marlon Brando

Many artists whose work has been recognized in the New York press can find themselves called out to Hollywood for inspection and possible employment. I think the most touching experience from my sojourn to LA was when I was asked to collaborate with Marlon Brando on a screenplay he was writing for young people about a boy and his pet bull.

I think I was asked because I do a lot of work with children and for children and, by nature, I am not someone who would have broken any of Brando's boundaries or tried to cash in on his name. Why would I? I'm basically an experimental composer and writer. I remember driving up to his house on Mullholland Drive and being touched by the simplicity and Asian quality of his living space. The first time I met him I had to wait three hours because he was swimming and getting a massage. I didn't mind, because, of course, he was Marlon Brando, and there was also something peaceful about his living room. He also supplied a legal pad and pencil where I was to sit. So I wrote down some of my ideas for the screenplay. When he emerged, he was at his heaviest weight and was wearing a sea-green muu-muu, but even so, his tremendous sexuality was not diminished. He had a power that was undeniable. And I could see why, when he was young, he made the impact that he did. He was also very kind and fragile. When we talked about the bull and the boy, he was extremely excited and made lots of references to gypsies, who fascinated him. He talked for a very long time about gypsies and homeless wanderers. He talked for about four hours with me barely saying a word, but I was never bored or resentful. He seemed to be like a child—as excited about what he was saying as anyone could be. We worked together and made a decent script, which Sean Penn was to direct. I flew in to hear a reading with Penn and Angelica Houston as the main gypsies, as well as other movie stars taking lesser parts. The only problem with the reading was that because they were film actors, not stage, they talked quietly into mics above their heads as they sat around a table in Penn's house. I couldn't hear a word from my chair on the sidelines. It was peculiar. But again, I must emphasize the graciousness of the people and their love for the script, noting that Sean Penn had done an extraordinary amount of research on bullfighting and gypsies. He showed me books and then more books that he was using.

The only problem with Marlon was that when I got back to New York, he had the habit of calling me on the phone at four-thirty in the morning, probably because of the time difference, or mostly because he lived in his own time frame in his own world. At first I didn't mind the phone calls, but he didn't want to talk about the script, he wanted to talk about whatever was on his mind. And I remember distinctly that one of our most memorable conversations was when he had just finished reading a book by Alice Walker and wanted to get my feelings about clitoridectomies. This was certainly odd in the middle of the night, and I had to wake myself up to discuss this painful and timely subject with any amount of coherency. He, on the other hand, was brilliant, had read much and was passionate, as if he had just discovered this behavior went on in the Third World. Eventually, the calls tapered off and his communication with me began to slow down until I heard from him no more. Now and then I got phone calls saying he was ready to do the movie, but then nothing happened. Still, I'm very grateful that I met the man and experienced his eccentric but not crazy personality. I feel a fondness and gratitude towards him because he was so invested in life. At least, when I was with him. Marlon Brando had more ideas than most people I've encountered or as many dreams as any man I've ever met.

V. Me

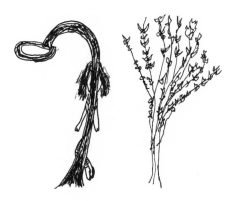

Camp Deer Run (2010)

The summers between 1958 and 1965 were uplifting and sane for me. I think they taught me what a healthy community of people might be like. I attended a summer camp in Sugargrove, Pennsylvania (near Jamestown, New York) called Camp Deer Run. It was owned by a Jewish couple, Bee and Sidney Alexander, who were the grumpy, sentimental parents of us all. I started when I was seven, and I never had a bad summer. We lived in log cabins according to our ages, Doe being for the youngest, and the deer names matured as we got older. The girls lived on one side of the camp and the boys on the other, separated by a huge lodge where we all ate common meals. The camp was highly ritualistic in its own strange way and gave me, more than did synagogue, an odd but totally believable sense of spirituality. The unique and terrific aspect of Deer Run was that, despite its Jewish leaders and big Jewish population, all rituals and games were based, supposedly, on American Indian myths, but I don't think very accurate ones. There was a reservation nearby and we traveled to it, yet saw no more than the "brave" dressed up for a price and loads of souvenirs made from beads and deer skin.

Of course I loved the drama and camp musicals, but for me the greatest challenge at the camp was canoeing. A camper began to learn from the first day the variety of strokes, how to sit in the bow, how to control from the stern. Once kids were strong enough, they were sent on canoe trips on the Allegheny River starting with one night out and building up to two weeks. Every year as campers got older they graduated to a longer trip. We'd paddle on the Allegheny, with the lush green woodlands on either side of us, until we reached a predetermined campsite, then set up the tents and pulled out the dishes and toilet paper and other necessities we'd been taught to pack. We learned how to dig a latrine and how to use one. How to light a fire—first with kindling and newspaper and then adding the various sized logs. I cherished the smell of the fire and the hot dogs we grilled and canned soups we boiled. I pretended we were of the forest and we'd skinned a bear. I learned to have a relationship to nature that I'd never had. My fantasy scenarios were full of Indian braves and ritual sacrifice, though a latrine was a latrine. Sleeping under the stars was my first potent drug. My body and the sky were comrades. That is why I think that, years later, I reveled when I traveled with Peter Brook's company and we were expected to camp out in the Sahara Desert. I found it blissful, whereas my companions complained of the coarse bulgy sleeping bags or of getting sand on their feet. I felt that same oneness that I had on the Allegheny River. A desert's worth of stars. The sweet loneliness of sleeping under an endless sky. The quiet of the night. The breath of wind going over my face. I was reminded of the canoe trips and was well prepared for a three-month camping out adventure in Africa.

Another aspect of camp which stayed with me my whole life was a sense of tradition and unspecific but strong religious rituals. There was a section of the camp where we were allowed only at certain times. It was a cleared out hill and field in the middle of the dense woods. The floor of the clearing was covered with pine needles. This was the campfire ground, and in the middle of this clearing was a large pile of logs that transformed into a blazing long-lasting fire. On campfire occasions, bunks of kids lined up single file and walked the distance to the clearing. Before we reached it, however, we passed a large tree called the Silent Pine, and once we passed Silent Pine, we could not talk. It was a time for meditation and concentration on nature. I could smell the pine in the air, and the silence opened my ears to the music of bird calls, insects, and frogs. It was eerie and beautiful. Once I entered the campfire site, I sat on the pine needle covered sloping hill and waited. Each week, a different bunk was chosen to light the tall tower of logs. The bunk that was picked made phony American Indian costumes out of pillowcases with holes cut for head and arms. The bottoms of pillowcases were cut to make fringe and symbols were painted on the "dresses," which were to bring up thoughts of "Indian" lore. Each camper in the bunk that was chosen was given a torch and, doing a special dance step and chant that I cringe about when I think of my Native American friends, campers approached from four sections of the forest to light the campfire. Once the campfire was blazing, a song was sung and the silence could be broken. If I think of it now, dressing in painted pillowcases and singing phony Indian songs is not only laughable, but politically abhorrent. But at the time, it had its own vague lovely spirituality and only the most skeptical could deny that a special beauty was given out by the tall pines and silent mountains.

At the end of each summer at Deer Run, we had a final ritual that I treasured. Each bunk was given a paper plate and each individual in the bunk was to write a wish or thought on the back of the plate. When dusk came, dressed all in white, we filed down to the shore of the lake and each of us melted the bottom of a candle and stuck it on the plate. At a given time, as the sky grew dark, we lit the candles and set the plates floating out on to the lake. Now there had to be more than a hundred candles floating gently on the lake out towards the center of the rippling water. Every year I was mesmerized by the sight and the presence of all those watching with me for whom I felt that kind of crazy summer passion. No one working in professional theater could have staged it better. (And by my last years at camp, there was the boyfriend of the summer with whom I could sneak off and neck.)

These simple corny gestures definitely informed the part of my brain that keeps looking for real spirituality. And I don't get too lofty about it. I hear it when a chorus sings a five-part harmony and I've felt it in a kiss now and then and seen it in the ruins of ancient civilizations, but Camp Deer Run, Sugar Grove, Pennsylvania, Bea and Buster Alexander, Weezie Shapiro (my trusted blood sister and friend) and Steven Blisky (my fellow kisser) are all essential elements in my being able to believe. It's awfully hard to find individuals or organizations to believe in, but I believe in the search, canoeing, and not being afraid of spiders.

Belief (2010)

As a child, Pesach (Passover) was a carnival to me. It was a dream of a circus starring my parents, my brother, my aunts and uncles and cousins. My mother had four sisters in varying shades of dyed blonde, red and brunette and there was a time when they were so close they didn't simply talk by phone but drove their cars five or six blocks to visit each other daily. No matter what Buffalo suburban tribal feuding might have been going on among them, all threats of vengeance were dropped for Passover. Matzoh ball soup was brought by one aunt, brisket by another, sweet potatoes with marshmallows melted on top by another, and they divided up the various traditional dishes of haroses, hard-boiled eggs and parsley.

My mother and her sisters were the dominant force for our Passovers. The uncles and my father didn't have a chance. I, on the other hand, was the youngest child of the youngest sister so I had a few years of playing the spoiled little princess. Covered like a leprosy victim with lipstick kisses all over my face, I took in a year's worth of love. I was to ask the four questions and I was determined to do it in a way that would do honor to my family and religion. I was also determined to find the afikomen (hidden matzoh) and bargain with my uncles for the highest price to give it back.

Most of my family was very quick and comical. When each sister got to read her portion of the Haggadah (Moses frees the Jews and brings them to the Promised Land), she competed fervently with her other sisters. Some improvised on the themes, some told terrible jokes, some read in Shakespearean voices or faked dying. My mother set the archaic prose to Gershwin tunes. It is the tradition to drink a glass of wine several times during the "service." The adults followed the text and a couple of my uncles added a few extra toasts. Every single adult at the table usually became a roaring drunk. They told stories about each other, teased the cousins, laughed until the five women looked like clowns with dripping mascara. Each uncle was like a Supreme Court judge reading his passages with grave seriousness and then providing an incoherent (and often lengthy) analytical commentary on the meaning of the whole night. But Passover wasn't simply a drunken party. It was also the closest we got to telling the story of our family's heritage and in between the joking and clowning were many unspoken reminders of the bad things that happened to Jews simply because they were Jews as well as being ghosts of lost grandparents, aunts and uncles.

I speak of Passover because by the time I was in my teens, various family tragedies diminished the crowd at the Seder table and the tone of the night became less riotous. By the time I was sixteen, there were no Seders and then I took off for college and became a serious artist at Bennington who didn't celebrate trivial holidays and certainly never went home. But as I grew into my thirties I realized that, of all the influences in my life, our Passover Seders were my first exposure to real theater and that they truly were the force that shaped my own eccentric version of what Judaism was. The phrase that was supposed to guide the whole holiday stayed inside me. My uncles always said:

"We are not free until every person in the world is free."

And that is why all people, particularly the poor and homeless, as well as clueless gentile friends, must be included. And the door was left open not just for Elijah but for the runaways all night. I don't think my relatives really believed that, but I fell for it, hook, line and sinker.

I'd lost my mother, brother, aunts and uncles at an early age and I survived and even flourished, but Passover turned out to be a particularly painful time for me. When I joined other families' rituals I only felt angry because they were so boring and sober (literally) and the language in the prayer books was dry and stilted, not like the language of my poetic improvisational family. Finally I stopped going at all. In rebellion I had hot dogs, Mexican or Chinese food. I blocked out the past.

Then I figured it out. I could make my own Passover. It would be a pageant in the free sense of the word. I set various texts to music telling the story of the Exodus and ended up with a full oratorio. My main source was Elie Wiesel's midrash on Moses and I met with him many times so he could give me a solid, real sense of the use of Biblical text. He was very kind and brilliant in the word of the Torah. I sang it for Joseph Papp as much as one voice can create a chorus in harmony and he was hesitant at first. He didn't want to put on a strictly religious piece of theater. That wasn't his image of the Public. But then I told him that I was burning to make a Seder for non-Jews, a holiday where people of all religions were stimulated to learn the reasons to be Jewish. It was the same as telling Jesus' story without asking the audience to become Christian. I figured if I had to sing the Hallelujah Chorus every year (with gusto) why couldn't non-Jews really experience what was joyous and fun and open and generous about being a Jew?

"No man shall be free until everyone is free."

I had a blast casting the oratorio. I hired a cantor, a lesbian rabbi, a troupe of gospel singers, rock 'n' roll artists with really gorgeous voices, a ninety-year-old Yiddish actor, a Puerto Rican salsa singer, Jewish and Christian friends who could wail and chant and dance, and four boys from a school that no longer exists who were exactly like the Boys Choir of Harlem, so I had four black boy sopranos. It was a carnival. A Jewish Mardi Gras.

And the touch that really gave the oratorio its shape and its wonder was a young, serious, wildly imaginative puppeteer named Julie Taymor. This was pre-*Lion King* but she had just the same brilliance. She created eerie shivering shadow puppets for the plagues. A terrifying Angel of Death. Her work wasn't just scary. Images for every step from Moses in the bulrushes along the way to the Promised Land. The Red Sea was flowing parachute silk. Pharaoh's army had a huge diabolical mask that had dancing soldiers to pursue the Jews. Her puppetry went perfectly with my music and although the piece was only seventy-five minutes, we even had an organized intermission where the audience stayed in their seats and were given matzoh while goofy rubber-faced puppets sat at their own miniature table and argued as to how many plagues there actually were (with the usual Jewish gossip and arguments added in).

After the matzoh we staged and chanted the Ten Commandments, the Golden Calf, the forty days in the desert. The cast sang and acted out the story in huge harmonies and dance-like movements. I wanted the roots of the music to come from all over the world. Jewish modes are not dissimilar from Indian ragas or the scales that guide the singers of the Koran, Flamenco music and even African, especially Ethiopian, chants. At the very end of our colorful adventures and sometimes scary pageant we brought in large tables and the cast sat down and had its own very simple Seder. The re-creation of the family's gathering consisted of prayers for understanding among all peoples. The boy sopranos sang "Arise my beloved, my fair one, and come away. The rain is over and gone." This was a text from the *Song of Songs,* which welcomed the spring and the relief and pride of surviving each person's dangerous or lonely winter. Survival, I believed, was also a strong theme in Jewish lore.

The oratorio was a delightful success and drew a wide range of audiences. We performed it three years in a row for the entire spring season and probably could've gone on for many more years. I was pleased, as always, to have a successful show, but most importantly, I had found a way to create an evening that brought back and even outdid my family's yearly carnival. And I found out that Passover was the main place I'd learned my limited knowledge of Jewish ethics.

After *The Haggadah*, I went on to create secular works—a jazz opera about a pimp who has to fight a prostitutes' labor union, a musical about a homeless person who sued Ed Koch and the City of New York, a true story, a play called *The Forty-Nine Years,* which addressed my mother's suicide, and on and on. But I also found that I was drawn to recreating Jewish stories that were religious in their roots but completely secular in their execution.

I did a version of *Esther* where Esther was Wonder Woman, and I also used magical illusions designed by Charlie Reynolds, who worked with many famous magicians, including Harry Blackstone. It is the tradition of Esther that magic and drinking prevail and you don't know good from bad or what's right from left. The rich become poor and the poor become rich. In this show my Jewish Wonder Woman conquered the weasely murderous bigot—Haman.

I found I was choosing Bible tales that could be made into secular spectacles, but also contained my own emerging liberal, leftist, humanist politics. I found in all the Jewish stories "midrashes" that taught the Jewish people to treat others decently and fight for the oppressed, whether it was their own people or others. I did many Bible tales. This replaced going to synagogue or consciously praying. But my cultural connection to my Jewishness seems to stay unswerving, though it's only through art and art alone.

One example of a successful mixture of elements was a version I did of Jeremiah's story in *Jerusalem*. In my interpretation, Jeremiah dashes to each of the warring sections of Jerusalem and warns the people that if they don't get along the whole city will burn. This took an enormous amount of work because I had to find all the inhabitants of my fictitious Jerusalem but the inhabitants had to be real representations of their culture and they all had to have beautiful voices.

In the Tri-State area I found:

1. Ethiopians
2. Roman Catholics
3. Arabic Muslims and Christians
4. Greek and Russian Orthodox Christians
5. Yemenites
6. Sephardic Jews
7. Ashkenazi Jews

Once again I found I needed a boy singer, but this time simply by accident he turned out to be a Mormon. There was a chorus made up of the usual rock and folk singers. The words for the Greek-like chorus came from the poet Yehuda Amichai. Each ethnic group expressed its beauty with its own music and then its anger with the other. Then cultures began to sing harmonies together and the "accidental" similarities and interlocking beats caused the feuding religions to take a second look.

The eclecticism of *Jerusalem* wasn't facile or arbitrary. My expertise is in world music and it is only in the last ten years that cultures are coming together and experimenting with mixing their instruments and modes. I believe the combination of a sitar and a pedal steel guitar is fabulous as is a singer from Mali accompanied by an Arabic drummer on doumbek. The same is true of a klezmer band applying its expertise to hip hop. I've been a part of this world since 1972 and strongly believe that these combinations stretch music and give us original and exciting sounds that we've never had before. I also believe the pure and excellent identity of each separate culture must be kept on its own so we have the benefit of the virtuosos on each instrument and use of their indigenous voices.

Jerusalem played in Lincoln Center Out of Doors, La Mama, the Old City of Jerusalem, as well as in opera houses in Italy and Germany, and I was asked to bring the production to my hometown of Buffalo. That was curious indeed. These fantastic voices coming together separately and as a choir was like nothing I've ever made. And the group, which had started out hostile and suspicious, stayed together performing for close to four years. They were proud of being an odd family.

So this was my Judaism. It was strong and I needed it. What made it Jewish was that I was a Jew. My choice of texts came from all sects and styles, but the Old Testament was the source of the stories. (I used the King James translation.) I went ahead to do *The Story of Job, Jonah, Song of Songs*, and a nonlinear piece called *Bible Women* where I took the women from the Bible and gave them the strength and humor I felt they deserved. I've done a piece based on non-Jews who hid families during the Holocaust based on a book by Eva Fogelman at the U.N. A piece about the partisans during the Holocaust was performed at the Holocaust Memorial Museum in Washington, D.C. On March 25, 2011, at Judson Church in New York City, my piece was presented in honor of the one-hundredth anniversary of the Triangle Shirtwaist Factory Fire where one hundred and forty-six women, primarily Jewish and Italian, were burned or jumped to their deaths.

There is a heavy dose of a Jewishness in *Missionaries*, the opera I wrote about the four churchwomen who were murdered and raped in El Salvador in 1980. When I heard about the deaths and the assassination of Archbishop Romero, I was shocked by the absolute inhumanity of the death squads and even more outraged because most people knew that the Reagan government and the United States military were supporting the dictator and providing for the American soldiers who were training the animals who committed these crimes.

I didn't make the piece immediately but waited several years and, even then, it took ten years and many workshops before the piece was in shape to show the public. But it had to be done.

I don't like the idea of people going into Third World countries and trying to convert them to anything, even a mild form of Christianity. I am put off by the wealth and corruption of the Catholic Church. As I write this now I have to deal with the fact that the current Pope was in Hitler Youth. I'm aware that for every white missionary or aid worker or doctor who gets killed there are millions of dark-skinned human beings dying from wars, famine and disease. So why did these four women get to me? I think I was in love with their absolute dedication to the poor without being holier than thou. They were four cool women who could've gone home anytime and didn't. They were passionate and feisty. One rode around on a motorcycle. Another nearly got into a fistfight with a soldier. They were terrified half the time and they kept on working. They continued to laugh and read beauty magazines and make fun of each other. Why else did I pick three nuns and a laywoman? Because as a Jew, every wrong against them specifically violated what I believe is the corruption of what religion is supposed to be about. And the women were down-to-earth heroes, not public figure or symbols of a master. I wanted to memorialize these women. It is a composer's job to honor the dead. Especially a Jewish composer. I wanted to tell their story and bring them justice. I believe that truth and justice are essential characteristics of my style of Judaism. Most of all I really believed in their believing. And in their joy. I go back to the Seder table in Buffalo, New York, and the four women and all the other righteous characters in my many shows sit with my family, get tipsy on wine and we all say:

"No man or woman shall be free until everyone is free."

"You Do the Math — I Couldn't Possibly" (2005)

I have to make a confession: I'm an idiot when it comes to numbers. This is a source of great humiliation. I can remember my first teacher, Mrs. Smith (that was her real name) leaning her long angular body over my desk. She wore severe grey hair styled in a flip, making a shadow of a vulture over my desk. "Are you all right dear?" The gentle growl from between her teeth as she examined my pages of printed numbers on the yellowish test paper and I'd shiver as if a voice could pinch. I lived in Buffalo at the time and the prestigious Albright Knox Art Gallery is built right near to where I grew up. It is very modern and very avant-garde and I visited it regularly with my father. Perhaps I was unconsciously creating a personal vision of abstract expressionism because my clunky numbers leaned over sideways, hung off each other, flipped upside down, leaned backwards, made little ships-Kewpie dolls. I missed twenty-seven days of first grade. I remember the exact number on my orange report card. (Though who can say any number I remember is exact.)

My parents said they had to keep going to doctors to blow out my sinuses, but that was just a cover-up. I was a nonstop whiner. I couldn't face Mrs. Smith. I couldn't face her blackboard covered with those evil twos and fours, pluses and minuses.

Eventually I learned to count, though I still make fists and my brain gets tight when I have to do it. I get by like my father who is colorblind, he's got a charming smile but if you look at his socks the illusion comes crashing into a chaos of greens and oranges. As I went through grammar school, each step along the way, addition, subtraction, long division was a crisis tantamount to the physical feats performed on Survivor (with the same fear of rejection). Long before any drug experimentation, numbers broke apart when I looked at them. They became funny like little animated sticks and circles. A kaleidoscope that laughed at me. Probably I have one of those learning disorders they now describe with each use of multiple syllables and prefixes. But when I was growing up there was no pity on the mathematically maimed.

Algebra nearly destroyed meals and my parents' cocktail hour. My father sat me down every night in his dark wood den and he, being a math genius, was sure he could pull me through the e=ex torture. As my twelve-year-old students say, "Not." Algebra was like gymnastics and I wasn't capable of keeping my balance on a stepladder—metaphorically speaking. We'd end up in these ferocious screaming matches like people trying to free a car that's wedged in a snow bank. Forward. Backward. Spinning wheels. After a while it became a rule that my father would not try to help me in math and not mention math and when I flunked math he was neither to glower nor be self-righteous. If he behaved, we got through dinner, perhaps a whole evening.

I went to a high school where you could go way past a "F" by getting an "FF," which I guess meant that you'd failed even at failing. I never got anything higher; I'd stare at my algebra book, waiting, literally, for a sign from God as to what all the signs and symbols meant. I prayed for religious voices to help me solve cosmic proofs. Anything. But alas, there was no math prophet. One of my girlfriends and I used to make frequent trips to the lavatory to pour water over each other's heads. We called it math purification. I spent freshman year very wet. The rest of my grades were impressive. My private school principal tried to figure out a solution so a few of us could graduate high school despite our plummeting averages. I thank him to this day. He recruited a sweet, oblivious woman who specialized in "slow learners" and threw all us double F's into a "special" chemistry class. The class was the joke of the school because we had oversized printing in big fat books, with lots of pictures. We did one experiment all year (mine had something to do with a hard-boiled egg) and, for Christmas, the teacher had us make little men out of marshmallows, toothpicks and cranberries. It's hard to believe, but my future depended on cranberries, toothpicks, and marshmallows. I managed to graduate and went to Bennington, which, luckily, at the time had never heard of math.

I think my darkest hour of numbers was the SAT, and I see this in girls I work with today (although they are more confident). The problems were indecipherable to me. I put aside the test packet altogether and concentrated on the answer sheet. Each question had an empty A, B, C, or D circle and you'd choose the one indicating the right answer and fill it in with your specialized pencil. I developed elaborate stories and rituals. "Well I've already done two 'As' so the 'C' is probably getting jealous – time for a 'C.'" "OK, so 'B' stands for banana and 'D' for doughnut and a banana is healthier than a doughnut so let's put down 'B,'" and so on . . . . My score came back in the low three hundreds. So much for the I Ching approach to the SAT.

Now I am a woman with a complicated and exhilarating career in music, theater and writing. I've composed many shows, movie scores, videos and concerts. I've written books and articles. I'm lucky. I've won awards, been trashed, resurrected, trashed, and mentored dozens of young artists. I've survived well. But I still clench my teeth and squint my eyes as my taxi drives up to its destination. "Oh my God, if the toll is 6.25 and I want to tip twenty percent, I have to figure out what ten percent of 6.25 is . . . We'll round it to seven. Ten percent of seven is seven—seven dollars or cents. Oh my God 1.40 plus 6.25 is—I don't know I don't know . . . seven something and I have a ten—a ten—OK so give him the ten . . . keep the change." Taxi drivers are delighted and shocked by sudden generosity or infuriated when I ask for change that's bigger than the fare. My friends grab for the check at restaurants just to avoid waiting for me to figure out my part of it. I'm probably one of the few college-educated women who still say "five take away three." This nasty secret accompanies me whenever I have to deal with numbers. It started as a problem and then years of embarrassments and *faux pas* have turned it into a panic. I know what's needed for every area of production, but I can't calculate the costs (What do you mean $5000 for snacks?). Luckily there are expert general managers to take over those tasks. I'm fastidious about earning a living and paying employees, but I don't know from day to day what my checking balance is. My finances as a whole are watched over by a business manager. He is the soul of goodness and we've been a team for thirty years, but he could embezzle every cent I own and I wouldn't know it until my cable got turned off (there's this niggling feminist discomfort in the fact that I'm letting a man do my finances, but asking him to have a sex change wouldn't cover my ineptness). I won't let stupidity get in the way of living a smart life. So I accept these crude limitations and come up with different formulas (ahaa) for surviving. I even rejoice in trying inventive compensations. I ask the taxi driver to "turn up that song, I really like it," so I can buy time while I'm stumbling through my calculations. I don't want to give into what is a stereotypical female handicap (though I know many men who flunked math, too). I'd like to know what happened. Somewhere along the way I think I got taught wrong. Addition is Mrs. Smith's thin stern lips. Subtraction her sad sigh. She didn't pass on the beauty of mathematics or the fun. I know that music is about the coming together of parts and the leaving, adding, and multiplying of sounds. You play with the disappearance of one quantity and the arrival of another. I'm a composer, my ears can comprehend the vast and quickly changing equations of rhythm and melody—so why can't my eyes understand the symbols on the page?

Despite developing a sense of humor, most math idiots carry around inside a feeling of being slightly damaged; less than whole. Only a percentage of oneself. When you're so bad at something, you might see the whole human engine as defective. I'm not going to get weepy or over-psychological here but the early days in school, the failure and humiliation have taken their toll in my overall confidence. I mean how can anyone be so *bad* at anything?

Am I hopeless or a victim of the teaching methods of the 1950s? Is it the chemical makeup of my brain or negative conditioning? To explore these questions, I've employed three young girls to be my private tutors. They get a costume jewelry bracelet of their choice for pay. Jordan is nine and a math whiz. Charlotte, her friend, is six and likes math fine. Lindsay, Jordan's six-year-old sister, won't talk to me very much at the beginning but every now and then pokes me, holding up a picture or diagram she's composed. Yes, I agree. Sometimes explanations are meaningless. Here we go. Already I discover that their school lives are very different from what mine was. When they do math, they sit down together in groups and help each other, boys and girls equal. Does that mean they cheat? I ask them. Eyes roll in unison. Cheat at what? Typical adult thinking. They sort blocks. Count on fingers. Straws. They have penny drives. They use jars and colored toothpicks. They make necklaces and use beads for addition, subtraction and multiplication by

146

sliding beads up and down. They have metaphors; if one rose equals five daisies, how many daisies are there in three roses? (Like a slot machine.) I get that. They draw pictures:

How many figures does this box have?   (Illustration 1)

Okay, 4.

If you color in one of the box it's ¼.

(Illustration 2)

I get that.

But then Jordan has this box with a hundred little boxes inside and she is filling in 18 of them and saying something about "18 percent."
I start to panic.
Lindsay nudges me and holds up a sheet of paper. "It's a tree," she said with both patience and disgust. She is either bored with me or doesn't like math that much and wishes we were doing art. Maybe I'm just projecting that. We both have red hair and brown eyes, she has an intense imagination. Maybe I want one of my tutors to be on my side.

They tell me that they can also learn math and history as one. Like Columbus started out on his voyage to discover America with one boat, then two boats followed – how many boats in all? Three, yes. I didn't want to say Columbus was an imperialist who paved the way for the assassination of entire Indian cultures . . . it didn't seem appropriate, but I got three! I got it without making fists.
In the course of this tutoring session Jordan tells me about her teacher who answers phone calls every evening from 5:30 to 8 to help any of her students with their homework. She won't talk to parents, just her students!
Charlotte says she gets to take off her shoes and gets ice cream at the end of the day.
All I remember is flash cards. Flash cards flashing too fast. And a

long blackboard with long numbers neatly printed. I'm inspired and moved by the girls' enthusiasm and ownership of their numbers. Their genuine sweetness isn't marred by tension and self-doubt. They are set to go against the boys. They will be ready for a world full of numbers.

Finally, I sit down with Tim, a student of mine from NYU. He majored in theater and mathematics. Now he teaches math at Stuyvesant High School, a brainiac school for science and math whiz kids. Tim is twenty-two and a math genius (he says he's not—he is in fact in the lowest grouping of the group that might one day do research) the 99.8th percentile or something. "No! Don't quote percentiles," he warns me. He also writes absolutely filthy, funny songs. (I wonder if there's a correlation.) "Math is all in the teaching" he says, "I could get you to do algebra in a week—I swear." And he tells me that culturally girls aren't taken seriously—"They fade out at about grade seven"— although his three favorite students are African-American girls who had to fight like hell to get into the school. He says math is "invigorating," "inspiring," it's about the "truth." It's like "working out." You want to find a solution, prove a solution. "You want to know the right way. The only right way." It's satisfying to prove that something's one hundred percent true. That's hard for me to grasp when my job is about the in-betweens, unsaids, unknowns, and mysteries. My young tutors, however, seem to grasp the pleasure of solving questions with absolute truth. When Jordan shows me a percentage of the squares to a big square, she is like Wonder Woman having saved a city. Her posture is that of a nine-year-old lioness. I like that. It means that, over time, teaching math has become more about the learners, even girl learners. Numbers are just something you use for math like the way you need colors for painting. The core of math can be an exciting personal voyage. Ever hopeful, I go off to count some shiny beads.

Bipolar Diaries (2007)

I hate this politically correct term—bipolar. On the surface it can seem sexy, like bicoastal or bisexual. Or it might suggest that I'm into saving the environment, traveling to those places where penguins mate and whales eat seals.

Bipolar.

I'm only too aware of how any clinical psychiatric term can brand a person. When the term was manic-depressive, the associations were somewhat romantic. Mad, feverish, dancing through the night to no music, buying out the women's department of a clothing store, even buying out the company, sleeping with the population of a whole town, cutting off an ear—in other words, life as loud and erratic as an out-of-time drum solo. Although many still believe an illness of this kind is brought on by what one of my relatives once called "spoiled brattedness," at least now science has shown it to be a serious brain disorder, as chronic as diabetes. And the newer bipolar is a little less hysterical, as in a woman who cooks and cleans all night and then can't get out of bed, or the quintessential diabolical boss, or the party-girl student out every evening, self-medicating with cocaine and alcohol until she drops. But even these images are off. Bipolar behavior isn't always so dramatic or public. Very often the sufferer functions quite well and struggles with the constant whiplash of mood in devastating privacy.

I, for instance, have started no world wars lately. I haven't bought a new wardrobe or physically attacked a singer who was out of tune. Nor have I ever missed a rehearsal or show, or stopped teaching due to my disorder. Only those closest to me know when I am thinking too fast, coming to drastic conclusions, imagining friendly atmospheres as threatening, or having to censor all the words that ricochet through my brain. Although there are still periods when I am pushed around by my moods, I've learned what I have to do to not succumb to bipolar disorder's more extreme symptoms.

Over twenty-five years ago, I was in my late twenties, weighing in at ninety-three pounds, talking as fast as an auctioneer, dashing from one activity to another with such intensity that I practically burned rubber.

I'd noticed since college that I could go for weeks on high energy, not sleeping, barely eating, and then I'd end up sick and utterly exhausted. But that was the rhythm of university life, right? Still, at twenty-seven, twenty-eight, my erratic energies weren't evening out. In fact, the dips and highs became more exaggerated. I was composing and writing a show in New York while working on my first novel. Everything, and I mean everything, was vital, essential, and urgent, and my obsession with work and relationships went beyond the outrageous self-absorption created by adolescent hormones. Weeks of frenetic activity, extreme intellectual and sexual passion, would result in a temper that could see me throwing a tape recorder out a window if a song wasn't going right. This razorlike edginess would be followed by the bottom dropping out: I wouldn't understand what all my energy had been for. I didn't know why I had cared so much about what I'd been caring so much about. I felt stupid and clumsy, unworthy, and doomed to a life of meaningless existence. In my shame, any thought that entered my head was aimed at letting myself know I was a failure in every measure of my person. When this happened I would hole up—isolate myself, and go out only for whatever work I knew I had to face. When I did go out, I'd fake interest and try to maintain the project and friendships I'd created as that seemingly completely other person.

After several years, these extreme back-and-forths took such a toll on me and were so confusing, I began to want only silence and the end of unpredictability. There were too many voices screaming and singing and whispering in my head. So noisy I used to count the layers of tracks going on at the same time. They praised and whipped at me. They mocked me and raised me to heights of unrealistic grandeur. They led me toward even more self-destructive behavior. And finally they exhausted my will. Luckily, I had several friends who insisted that I see a psychiatrist.

At first when I spoke to the doctor it was as if I were auditioning for the role of a nineteenth-century poet. I talked about how I felt the power of the gods and the ominous presence of danger at the same time. I thought I was possessed with a heavenly vision, and yet I was unworthy and incapable of keeping up with the greats of history. I needed sex. I hated sex. I was a vampire with no libido. I was a savior of humanity with no friends. I understood the deep symbolisms of shapes, numbers, colors, and letters, but I barely had the energy to spell or add.

After listening to my tirades, the psychiatrist asked me if I had ever considered taking medication. I was stunned and extremely skeptical. I'd watched my mother slowly deteriorate into a woman who lay on the couch for hours. I never could erase her slurred speech from my head. I didn't know what drugs she'd been on, but they made her bloated and dull. I knew certain psychiatric conditions could be passed on, and my mother's downward slide, as well as the mental illnesses of several other family members, haunted me. Was there a genetic strain that I could do nothing about? I dreaded being paralyzed as she seemed to be, or labeled. Medication equaled cowardice to me, the height of luxurious narcissism. Didn't drugs wipe out creativity? Didn't medicine take away your sense of humor and neutralize you? I thought of Aldous Huxley's *Brave New World*. I would be one of a nation of lazy do-nothings addicted to the "happy drug" soma. How could I help rectify the problems of the world if I had to take pills? I really went on and on about this. My noisy brain burst with more tracks berating myself for even needing to consider the possibility of medication. Illegal drugs were much cooler. Bob Dylan never wrote a song called "O Lithium" or "Antidepressant Blues."

Because of my opposition to medication, life continued to be agony. I never knew who I was going to be in the morning, and my reactions to everyday events continued to crash, clang, and resonate in my brain like a huge Japanese gong. I came very close to suicide, and since the final chapter of my mother's story had ended exactly that way when I was twenty-three, I felt in danger. Now in my late twenties, I realized that I loved life enough to be terrified of following her actions. I finally decided to take the risk.

For the first two years, I would go on medication, then abandon it. The idea of needing drugs still seemed proof of a kind of failing that I had trouble facing. I wanted to be able to control my inner demons and not be "ill." And I hated the thought of chemicals playing with my brain. So in the beginning I was constantly monitoring myself: Was that a dull observation? Is the melody I wrote less edgy than two years ago? Was that not funny, and if it wasn't funny, is it because I'm drugged? Have I been quiet for too long? Am I becoming a cow?

As it turned out, the medication hardly turned me into a zombie. Instead it cleared some of the noise in my head and helped replace the feeling of relentless inevitable doom with a shaky determination to join the rest of the human race in the basic day-to-day ups and downs of life. As the poet Nazim Hikmet writes, "Living is no laughing matter: / you must live with great seriousness / like a squirrel for example— / I mean without looking for something beyond and above living, / I mean living must be your whole occupation." For me it was definitely quite a job, but at least with medication I had the will to struggle.

I was lucky enough to find a doctor who was part scientist, part alchemist, and part shaman, while being up on the latest medical discoveries and courageous enough to try continual adjustments in treatment. This was also a doctor who listened to me. I found it unacceptable to be overdrugged, for example—to lose access to the energy that connected me to those I worked with who kept me creative in my pursuits. In order for the doctor to help me, I had to be able to describe with extreme accuracy what I was feeling. I also saw a therapist who showed me how to clarify what was chemical and what was not.

Slowly I was able to teach myself to ignore the bad voices, because they were softer and not so insistent. I could think twice about a reaction to another person or event now that the reaction didn't happen so instantly I couldn't do anything about it. I learned to watch myself going through an impulsive or manic action and stop myself before that one snowballed into another— and another and another. The high court of my brain didn't judge me, or others, quite so severely. Often it was hard to know—and still is—whether my reactions were legitimate or tainted by chemical imbalance. But time and experience continue to teach me to understand my mood changes and how to differentiate an emergency from a simply lousy day.

Most important, therapy has guided me over the years in learning how to "behave well." One of my rules now is that regardless of the situation, there is no reason whatsoever to impose my inner storms on others. It's perfectly okay to let someone know I'm having trouble or to confide fears in a trusted friend, but to act out a misguided interpretation of an event, or to impose a rush of anger on another person, is destructive and has consequences. It reads well to have a madwoman trashing her apartment, getting into a fistfight with a saleslady, and, of course, staring down at the bottom of a whisky glass with cigarette smoke swirling into the neon lights of an all-night bar. It reads well to have the mad lady not eating for months, writing pages of incoherent poetry, or calling friends at four in the morning to discuss the meaning of life. Yet in reality, even the most outrageous rock 'n' rollers, poets, and anarchists get bronchitis, lose jobs, alienate friends and come too close to doing themselves in for very little purpose. So learning to behave may seem prissy, but in the long run, life to me offers much more vibrant, important moments of discovery and light because I've gained some semblance of self-discipline, dignity, and privacy about my problems. While being rather strict with myself, however, I do try to hear those close to me when they remind me that I am one of many who suffer from a real disorder. I am not a freak. I am not "wrong." And I'm certainly not unique.

Let me be honest. Even with medication and therapy, nothing has been "fixed." I am not "cured." Living with this disorder is a continuous virtual sports tournament. There are so many images that come to mind: tightrope walking, bullfighting with powerful snorting moods, or sometimes it's like my mind is still a breathless animal panting through an agility course. It burrows into tunnels, leaps over walls, pushes turnstiles, keeps my endurance up just enough so I can barely make it to a last free, open run in the field. And that run ultimately ends, like a Road Runner cartoon, falling off a steep cliff.

One difficult reality of the bipolar condition is that the medicines may need to be changed or adjusted quite often—sometimes even within the same year. Certain drugs can stop working, or they cause side effects when combined with others. For instance, one gave me the shakes. I switched to another and my mind went back to zooming and careening. You find sometimes that without an antidepressant, a mood stabilizer will push you into the muck of depression. An antidepressant without a mood stabilizer can send you flying dangerously. And side effects include severe anxiety and headaches.

It takes a certain kind of patience to put up with this perpetual game of musical meds. At one point, I got incredibly discouraged and angry. I felt like a toxic waste dump. I scolded myself that I was no more than a downtown avant-garde version of Jacqueline Susann's *Valley of the Dolls*, although it wasn't true. And since I never missed a work appointment or deadline, I couldn't help but think: If there are so many moments when, despite my problems, I can focus, maybe I don't need medication at all. Like most people burdened with bipolar disorder, too, I was very sensitive to others who think we are addicts taking the easy way out. So, in my frustration, I decided to stop all medication. Clean out.

It was a disaster. After a couple of weeks my mind became a protest march with all the different contingents demanding their rights. There was nonstop commentary from a newscaster telling me that I must do this, I must do that, get to this, get to that, not be like this, start right now, stop it! Pundits gave opinions on the judgments of the newscaster and fights inside my brain broke out that were worse than anything on *The View*. All the mania put me on the brink of total exhaustion, and the whole situation was made worse because I knew I was irrational and had to direct myself moment by moment like a drill sergeant to behave normally, say the right things in conversation, and even just lift a glass of water to my lips without shaking. Inevitably, of course, after the violent waves of energy, I ended up fighting a depression so thick that for weeks it felt like I was moving through a solid bog of grayish Jell-O. Most devastating of all, here was absolute proof I needed medication, and that caused me great shame.

Then came the fear. What if this was it? What if there was no medicine left to calm me down or dig me out? No way to regain a semblance of quiet or of light? Was I going to end up old and crazy pushing a shopping cart filled with Robert Johnson CDs and torn workout clothes?

The answer is no. Once I resumed medication and found even newer combinations, my rapid mood cycling eased, which has given me more time to take in the small gifts life has to offer. I can even experience a quietness now and again. A restfulness, and more and more often, all the tracks in my brain harmonize and there is joy.

I have also discovered other ways to help stave off the mania and its

154

dreaded other side, absolute despair. The list is somewhat boring but extremely essential. First, I must take care of myself physically—eat well, keep hydrated, and exercise. Second, I try to go outside as much as possible and absorb the life around me by watching—anything from dog walkers and young couples to skateboarders and hip-hoppers with iPods dancing out the beats. A crucial part of my survival is to take solace and pride in my work because it reminds me of who I am. It also reminds me of my vital connection to all the actors, singers, and writers who keep me focused. I buy books, go to movies, socialize, stay abreast of the news and culture—in other words, I try to keep myself in the world, away from the captivity of my mind.

Another form of relief is to read about my disorder, including the latest research. And I've learned to write down descriptions of my mind's travels and perceptions when I am in certain moods to help me remember that all of this has happened before, and whatever is torturing me will pass. Finally, I look to the wisdom of those who have seen me through the bad cycles and can tell me that they love me any which way I am.

In the last several years, scientists have made incredible progress in treating bipolar disorder, and today there are many more choices for mood stabilizers and antidepressants. I have been on a fairly consistent combination of drugs for a while now without any overwhelming side effects. And I can cautiously say that, for quite a long time, I've been able to claim my days and haven't had to be a constant mediator between my moods. I'm not about to bring out the bells, strings, and drums just yet, but I do have more good days than bad—and even the bad days aren't lost in hours of battling frantic energies or the deadweight of mania's reciprocal depths.

As I write this, I think about those who are just beginning the treacherous rollercoaster ride and, for anyone who hasn't found methods to help restore evenness and calm, I want to say: Hold on tight. Move slowly and with hope. Even if you are in the most chaotic state of mind or the most deadly despair, trust in time. Help is on the way.

VI. Waiting

Waiting (2008)

I am usually early for appointments, meetings, and gatherings. And I then have to wait. What is the appropriate time to ring the bell or sit down at the restaurant table? Often I am so early that I have to walk around the block a few times before I pretend to arrive. I have walked around many blocks in cities all over the world. I often tell myself that I spend too much time waiting. I used to be embarrassed when I sat alone in a restaurant for a breakfast. I've sat next to many quilted Teddy bears in overalls or squirmed on light wooden benches waiting for friends who are usually late by habit. This doubles or triples my minutes of waiting. What do waitresses think of me? (Notice that they are called "waitresses.") Do they think I have nothing else to do, that I am the person in the friendship who is less employed or more needy? I often thought that waiting puts me in an unfavorable light. A real woman would arrive five minutes after the called time, hair blowing in the wind, slightly breathless, buttoning the last button on her silk shirt as she tries to scan one more time the fax sent from Brazil, the note her lover left her on the bathroom sink, or her most recent journalistic article on the secret interview she had with a Middle Eastern politician whose name I can't pronounce. Or perhaps she was stuffing her children into snowsuits sending nanny husband strollers in a flurry as she checks the veal she's been marinating for two days to make some French dish whose name I also can't pronounce. Do I appear shiftless to my waitress with too much time to sit and do nothing? Does it mean I have too much time on my hands if I'm worrying about all this? The same discomfort is true when I wait outside offices. "She must really want that job. She's overly anxious—pushy. She was dismissed from her last job and is determined to do better." I've tried leaving my house much later for dates and meetings, but, even if I leave my house at what to me seems like a cliffhanger of a last moment, I end up waiting. I am not a capable last-minute diva; I'm a goody-goody. In recent years I've learned to bring a book, but I don't read it, or a notebook in which I rarely write. How lucky are the poets who sit in cafés lost in meter, rhyme, and profanity. Bare-naked waiting seems to be my plight. And when I wait, I am unable to distract myself. For instance, I don't watch TV or listen to my iPod on the treadmill. I watch every single red digital number pass to the next. I keep myself in agony knowing exactly how far I've gone and how far I have to go.

I think I started waiting very early on. I can remember standing by my window on Nottingham Terrace in Buffalo, New York watching each set of headlights as they sped past our somewhat spooky ivy-covered brick house. Every night I waited for my parents to come home. In the beginning there was no inside narration that I remember, but as I became five, six, and seven, I told myself that they'd never come home from that so-called party, or that their new Buick had plunged into Delaware Lake. I'd remember the well-publicized incident of the babysitter killer who knifed the little girl for whom she was sitting. I knew there were gangs of flesh-eating pirates in the attic and chains and campfires in the basement. I waited in desperation. I couldn't even get into bed until I heard my parents' car door slam (and I knew its pitch perfectly—if it had been any other car I'd have detected it instantly).

Waiting seems to be a universal activity. I've thought about making a picture book about that state of being. I'm overwhelmed by how we wait and what we wait for. Bingo numbers, election returns, on line at the meat counter, waiting for Aunt Herta to stop talking, for the plane to become first in line so we can take off, for a prescription at the pharmacy, for a poop in the potty trainer, for letters of acceptance from college, waiting, grinding your teeth in a traffic jam, waiting for a person's name to surface as you stand there with them holding your frozen smile, waiting for a skirt to go on sale, for the weather to get cooler or warmer, for the number on the scale to go up or down, for the cute person to look at you, for the creep to leave you alone, for your lover to get his divorce, for the cold to go away, for grades to be posted to see if you've passed, for a pain to pass, for gas to pass, for gas prices to go down, for vacation, graduation, for Friday at five, for midnight on New Year's Eve, for the baby to be born, waiting to be born, waiting to see if you got the loan, waiting for your child to come home from a dance class, college, a date, waiting for a marriage proposal, for the right time to turn it down, for the check, for the change—financial or hormonal, for the right words, for the laughter you hoped to get, waiting to hear that a crime has been solved, for an apology, for the reluctant smile, for your state's lottery numbers to be yours, waiting to be caught, waiting to see if you'll be caught, waiting to surprise someone, to delight, to make furious, waiting to be old enough for this or that and waiting for justice, or at least revenge, recognition, waiting for calm, for sleep, for a good night's sleep with no dreams.

As you can see the list goes on and on. We are creatures that wait or try not to wait or who dare not to wait or who are willing or unwilling to wait. We depend on time whether it's relayed on a digital watch, a stopwatch, a sundial, or acute inner timing. It seems that there are times in life where waiting is the foremost preoccupation. For instance, a dramatic time for waiting is when you are a female in adolescence. I was in such a hurry to see proof of my womanhood. I waited for breasts—would they ever fight themselves out of my flat chest? I screened myself for the one hair under my arm or the first pubic hair. I recently reread a fifth grade diary of mine where I was begging God to give me my period so I could be an adult (before my girlfriends, or at least not behind). I can also think of a few times where as a young woman I waited just as fervently for that same period to please come. Please make me not pregnant. The opposite is just as true. I have a friend who waited and waited, and tried all the modern scientific formulas to have a baby. She finally got pregnant at forty-five. Was there ever a more welcomed baby? Perhaps, in the bible, Sarah "waited" ninety years before she could have Isaac.

For both women and men, the phone is the essential instrument of waiting. I watch in rehearsals, at restaurants, in between classes as people check their cell phones. They check and check as if the motion is a nervous tick. We all have been phone sick. When I was fourteen I sat next to my pink telephone, walked away from it, went out of the room, came back, folded clothes, played the guitar, sobbed, slammed at my pillows, waiting and waiting and trying not to wait for the phone to cry out that one life-changing ring from a boy. It is a basic rite of passage to spend nail-biting moments staring pleadingly at a phone—landline, cell, satellite or pay phone.

For instance, in eighth grade I met Richard at Mindy's and necked with him a bit in her father's den. After that afternoon, my waking life was spent in waiting for him to call. I asked myself if I'd been too fast, too loose, too much, too little and would he call, would he call, would he call? He eventually did and my joy was out of proportion. I was in my wedding gown, beaming into his eyes all through the conversation. But in reality was he worth all that gut-wrenching waiting? That's another question about waiting—when is it real or when is it a one-woman show of angst and coffee? Now with e-mail and instant messaging you don't wait as long, but you do wait. How is the person going to evolve? What will he or she be like face to face? Does a long wait make romance more interesting or does it give you too much time? I wonder about World War II brides and girlfriends, the women and men of any war who wait three years for a loved one to come home. They must obsess and prepare for that one person who has been the subject of all their longing. This must be a complicated waiting period whether it's World War I or Iraq. The imagination creates characters and scenarios that often don't exist. When soldiers are at war, who actually is remembered accurately, and who gets recreated from scratch? My father went to Germany a short time after he and my mother were married. By the time the war was over, he'd been gone as long as he knew her. It's not hard to become strangers. You can create a fictional relationship. One time I had the opportunity to be able to meet a musician I worshipped. He was a great, legendary drummer. As I waited for our meeting, I heard myself singing in his band, I was having his children. Together we saved the world. But when I finally met him he was monosyllabic and twitchy. He didn't make eye contact and pounded on the table constantly. His legs jiggled up and down. He had one of those scratchy laughs that come out "heh heh"—all whiskey and mockery. He was probably wasted. For years after that I stopped liking his music. But it wasn't his fault he was who he was. No! I had created him in a fit of waiting.

Again the opposite kind of event can take place. Once a friend asked me to listen to the songs of a nephew. I dreaded the moment. As I sat in my loft waiting for the kid to arrive, I imagined nasal-sounding songs about life's cruelties when one is so young and so metaphorically abused. Or, I visualized a worse variation—he'd jump up and down stabbing at his reverberating guitar singing like an overly miked motorcycle. I was too tired to hear some kid screech, "die mother----er die." But it turned out that he was a very funny songwriter with a sweet melancholy, and I was smitten. Not only did I want to cast him in a show but I also wanted to adopt him.

As children we're taught to wait, count the days for holidays like Christmas and our own birthdays. Christmas is in December and consumption revs up starting in August. In the U.S. we've invented enough holidays to keep shoppers in action all year long. But Christmas is the grand finale. Our attention obsesses around giving and getting gifts. On the morning of Christmas (or eve of Chanukah) we sit down, untie or pull at a curly ribbon, remove the Scotch tape off of the tightly wrapped paper, try not to rip the wrapping paper but tear at it anyway and "poof" it's a pair of panty hose or a cheese basket— dog robots, a sweater, or a blender. Maybe, as they say, the gift is in the giving, but think of the amount of mental and physical energy spent on buying gifts, wanting gifts, and returning gifts. What are we waiting for when we look at those wrapped boxes? Maybe they carry our childhood dreams inside them. We wait for evidence of a special time or for a unique expression of love. Or maybe we just like *things*. Think of wedding and baby showers. The Macchu Pichu of gifts piled high waiting to be opened.

There are, however, pure moments worth the waiting. A great concert that has been advertised all year on the radio turns out to be better than the CDs. We smell rich chocolate coming from our kitchen and we know there are one-of-a-kind brownies waiting for us. We stand at a door at the airport and are thrilled when we see the face of the person for whom we waited. And we are newly in love by the time our lovers reach our doorstep. In our minds we have already kissed, embraced them, rolled around with them, undressed them, applied fragrant oils…and whatever else. When the real life person turns up at the door, he or she is everything we waited for.

Individually, we have different experiences of waiting that make our own lives what they are. Parents wait with curiosity to see their children emerge as people. Artists wait for each separate stroke of paint to become a whole. I wait for my dogs to relieve themselves instantly in below-freezing weather. A gardener waits in spring for what was planted in autumn. We wait for the verdict in the mirror as to how stunning we'll look in our new jacket. For the raise. A promotion. For a moment on the beach. A moment to do nothing. I wait for music to come into my head—music that gets me humming out loud like a flesh and bone calliope. A male friend of mine waits every Sunday at the flea market for objects to call to him.

I also think about the experiences of waiting that simply have to be endured. Time seems like it is your foe. I would, for myself, include mornings before the sugar of my orange juice to hit (my version of coffee). I watch a friend waiting for her colicky baby to stop crying. I believe she's on the waiting list for sainthood. Waiting for pain to go away is no small kind of waiting. Serious pain slows time down. The worse the pain, the slower the time. My friend has migraines and sometimes has to lie in a dark and silent room for hours. Pain makes waiting intolerable. And the pain or sickness of someone close heightens the anxiety of waiting. This is where prayers and bargains with God come in. Praying is an exercise of waiting. Waiting in the hospital waiting room while your father has heart surgery, waiting to hear about a friend who smashed up his motorcycle. All of it seems like endless empty time that can't get filled. Waiting can be a scary isolating experience. But I've also seen even the most alienated families lay down their weapons in a hospital waiting room. Waiting soothes tempers, offers perspective. Waiting or not waiting is our current word for if we should've gone to war. Together a country or world waits for the outcome of a disaster or the word on a leader. Television is a tool for waiting. As we wait for the outcome of an election, we are waiting to see which smooth-talking politician will be elected so he or she can ask us to wait for the economy to get better. We wait to be safe.

There are different methods and techniques for some waiting. I know someone who recited all the words to all the Beatles songs as she waited for her husband to come out of surgery. As far as I'm concerned, that's praying. Some of us have to wait for a diagnosis. The sitting room of a mammogram office is a place where you feel the act of waiting in the air. Sometimes the cheapest most gossipy trash papers help pass the time. Sometimes a choice of music on the iPod. There's the opposite attitude too. I have friends who get right on the internet or get Merck's Encyclopedia and rename every detail of their disease or possible surgery and either put themselves in a blind panic or feel stronger knowing all factors. Some of us face death or think we do when awaiting serious medical information. Some of us read wise teachings and others go stupid. Waiting for the results of a biopsy I found myself weeping over an order of macaroni and cheese thinking I'd never be able to eat it again if the tests came back positive.

There's even a superstition that if you don't wait, terror won't come or joy will come faster. I think of brave people who have to wait hours or days to be rescued. When I think of the scientists stuck in Antarctica waiting for a blizzard to pass or refugees waiting in leaky rubber boats for the right kind of current, or people standing on their rooftops in New Orleans. I know that these individuals are called upon to have extraordinary powers of waiting. I think we call it patience but the word should be stronger. Are there layers of the psyche that get stripped to the core as waiting goes on longer and longer? Waiting often requires courage. Or denial. Or belief. Waiting can be dangerous too. Soldiers wait for the signal to attack, to drop bombs. Terrorists wait years to activate a plan. Moses couldn't wait a second so he grabbed the bright hot coals and stuck them in his mouth. He stuttered from then on. We wait to see how long it takes to heal. Yes we humans are always waiting. Small waiting. Big waiting. Waiting to stop waiting. Animals wait too—we don't know what goes on in their minds. Scientists are waiting to find out ways to make new animals. Girraphants or Bearatoos.

When I was a child I used to sneak to the park across the street and, in the autumn, bury myself up to the neck in leaves. I felt, in my leaves, that I was in an igloo of sorts or a teepee. This special place I inhabited was the perfect spot for the miracle to happen when it did. I didn't know what miracle I was waiting for or even that I was waiting for a miracle, but I knew I was waiting. And I couldn't help but feel thrilled.

As I sat in that pile of leaves I waited, because something was certainly going to happen. I was never disappointed when it didn't. I knew even then that miracles come later. Sometimes you have to wait—if you're wearing leggings and you have to pee. I've also learned to stop waiting for some hopeful dreams. For instance, for my parents to change. To be able to fly. To do a backbend. Sometimes I wait to stop waiting. Is waiting a luxury? Is it stabling? Is it necessary or a mystical state? Religions wait for Sons of God, the Messiah, the Rapture, Nirvana and so on. We could say waiting is, not a religion, but a kind of faith. Or lack of faith if you happen to be waiting for the wrong person and that prince never arrives. So now I will not wait any longer to find the end to this piece. And you must be ready for me to finish it. Waiting can be as casual as it is profound. And there are times when it's absolutely time to stop waiting.

When I was a teenager, all I wanted to be was a grown woman. While I was waiting my wish came up behind me way too fast. We have to live in the present. Cherish the now. But watch out. You may start waiting to live in the now. And then it is gone. Whoosh! There it went.

Acknowledgments

Grateful acknowledgment is made to the following publications in which these works previously appeared: "The Story of a Street Person" *The New York Times*, August 18, 1991; "Stretching Boundaries: The Merlin of La Mama" *The New York Times*, October 26, 1986; "Job: He's a Clown" *Out of the Garden, Women Writers on the Bible*, edited by Christina Büchmann and Celina Spiegel (Ballantine, 1995); "Bipolar Diaries" *O, The Oprah Magazine*, October, 2007; "You Do the Math—I Couldn't Possibly" *O, The Oprah Magazine*, January 2005; "Waiting" *Hanging Loose 93*; *Listening Out Loud* (Harper & Row, 1989); *At Play: Teaching Teenagers Theater* (Faber and Faber, 2006); *The Four of Us* (Plume, 1993).

"Seven Laments for the Fallen in the War," by Yehuda Amichai, translated by Ted Hughes, *Amen* (Milkweed Editions, 1987).
"Four Quartets," by T.S. Eliot (Mariner Books, 1968).

I would like to thank my incredible editor, Donna Brook, without whom this entire book would not exist, and also Robert Hershon, my champion and hero of poetry, for his faith in my words despite the fact that my spelling is atrocious. Special thanks to Dick Lourie who helped untangle knots and webs. I would like to thank the fabulous team of Rebecca Keren, Matthew Robert Gehring and Preston Martin for technical assistance and moral support. I'd like to thank all of the magazines and journals that published the works that appear here, and special thanks to Marie Carter, Mark Pawlak, Kiyomi Dong, Celine Keating, and Miyako Hannan. And finally, to Roz, for all of it.